AUDIO CASSETTE ALBUMS

by Dr. T.L. Osborn

HEALING THE SICK — LIVING AUDIO CLASSIC EDITION
12-CASSETTE ALBUM — 12 HOURS OF MIRACLE POWER
RECORDED BY THE AUTHOR

YOU ARE GOD'S BEST — COMBO-ALBUM
152-PG. BOOK PLUS AUTHOR'S 4-CASSETTE RECORDING
(7/60 COLLECTION VOL. 1 — 18 CHAPTERS)

FAITH TO CHANGE YOUR WORLD — 5-CASSETTE ALBUM
    1 — THE UPLIFT OF BELIEVING — YOUR ROOTS
    2 — ON TARGET WITH GOD — YOUR PURPOSE
    3 — DYNAMIC LIVING — YOUR WELLBEING
    4 — SUCCESS UNLIMITED — YOUR PROSPERITY
    5 — LOVE POWER — YOUR SUCCESS SECRET

SUPER LIVING — 5-CASSETTE ALBUM
    1 — DISCOVERY FOR RECOVERY — YOU
    2 — THE GIFT WITH A LIFT — YOUR LIFE
    3 — THE FLARE OF BEING AWARE — YOUR HEALTH
    4 — WISE UP AND SIZE UP — YOUR MONEY
    5 — TO KNOW YOU IS TO LOVE YOU — YOUR POWER

POWER OF POSITIVE DESIRE — COMBO ALBUM
288-PG BOOK PLUS AUTHOR'S 4-CASSETTE RECORDING
(7/60 COLLECTION VOL. 3 — 50 CHAPTERS)

SAY "YES" TO GOD'S SUCCESS — 2-CASSETTE ALBUM

BIG LOVE PLAN — COMBO-ALBUM
184-PG BOOK PLUS AUTHOR'S 4-CASSETTE RECORDING
(7/60 COLLECTION VOL. 2 — 24 CHAPTERS)

See information on quantity discounts — page 6.

OSBORN CRUSADE - Benin City

Publisher

OSBORN FOUNDATION INT'L
Box 10 Tulsa, OK 74102 USA

Australia: Box 54, GPO, Sydney, NSW 2001
Canada: Box 281, Adelaide St Post Sta., Toronto M5C 2J4
England: Box 148, Birmingham B3 3EQ
New Zealand: Box 3442, GPO, Wellington

DEDICATED

To the Partners of our world ministry whose faithful support has enabled Daisy, my wife and me to tell people that God values them, that He is not mad at them, and that the price He has paid for them is the proof of their worth.

Crusade Photographs by
Dr. Daisy Washburn Osborn

T.L. OSBORN

Bible quotations in this book have been per-
sonalized, and sometimes synopsized to
encourage individual application. They are
derived from King James Version unless
otherwise noted. *The Author*

ISBN 0-87943-031-1
Copyright ©1986 by T. L. Osborn
Printed in the United States of America
All Rights Reserved

Contents

T.L. and Daisy Osborn keep their bodies fit by exercise and healthy habits so that they may live long and fruitful lives, sharing the gospel with millions around the world.

Dr. T.L. Osborn
Dr. Daisy Washburn Osborn—
on the GO, on the RUN to share
Christ with their world.

OSBORN CRUSADE—Kinshasa

YESU NASIYA BOE

THE OSBORN MINISTRIES

share the uplifting gospel of Christ with millions worldwide.
Their literature is published in 132 languages, their films
and teaching tapes in 67 languages, distributed FREE
around the world to help Christian workers reach
the unreached with the good news of God's love.

T.L. and
Daisy
Osborn
pray daily
for each
partner
and friend
who shares
with them
in reaching
out to help
people.

Introduction

by Drew Graham

*A*T A TIME when many ministers and churches were desperate for new ways to draw sinners into their sanctuaries to hear the Gospel, T.L. Osborn produced a classic, aimed at getting Christians ON THE GO . . . winning sinners, **out where they are.**

When some were ready to close up the church shutters and concentrate on "feeding the flock until Jesus comes," T.L. Osborn's book, "Soulwinning" — **OUT WHERE THE SINNERS ARE**, was sent, with the compliments of the Osborns, to over 100,000 pastors, missionaries and evangelists around the world.

Today there is scarcely a city or nation where someone is not excited about the resurgence of personal evangelism.

Groups and organizations of joyful soulwinners — lay men and women — are ON THE GO everywhere with the Gospel.

Mr. Osborn's first rallying call was for soulwinning — **OUT WHERE THE SINNERS ARE**. Then he wrote this book, the natural sequel to that call. This one cries for Christians to get ON THE GO — **OUTSIDE THE SANCTUARY**. It presents a series of lectures given by Rev. Osborn in his Soulwinning Institutes across the world. It places in clear, concise terms those secrets which T.L. Osborn has shared with so many thousands of fellow soulwinners.

As Christian laymen rediscover apostolic soulwinning ministries, and get on the go **OUTSIDE THE SANCTUARY**, Mr. Osborn believes they will write the last glorious chapter of the Church in action.

May the basic truths of these lessons inspire you to go OUTSIDE THE SANCTUARY and share Christ with those who will never go to church; may they help you to win a harvest of souls — in your own area and wherever you **go with God!**

1
JOIN
THIS
CHARIOT

*T*HE COVER illustration of this book depicts Philip, a Bible-day Jesus-man, talking about Christ to a celebrity traveling to Ethiopia (Acts 8:26-40). The fellow accepted salvation right there on the big public highway and became a believer.

This is what happens when a Christian is ON THE GO . . . OUTSIDE THE SANCTUARY.

This is taking the Gospel out where the sinners are, out where the action is.

This is putting the Gospel where it belongs . . . out on main street, on the broad highways and boulevards of humanity, out in the public places.

This is putting the Gospel on wheels, in action, into motion — hooking it up to transportation, mounting it on board vehicles, Gospel Cine-Vans and Gospel Cine-Boats, speeding it on the wheels of modern technology, on multi-color web presses, on the spools of magnetic and video tape and motion film.

This is putting the Gospel within reach of the

masses, where the poor can hear as well as the rich, where both beggars and merchants can partake together out along the public traffic ways, via the mass media, where millions who will never go to church, can hear about Jesus **outside the sanctuary**.

This was what God was saying to Christians of all times when he said to Philip: "GO JOIN THIS CHARIOT" v. 29. Hitch up the Gospel witness to every modern, mechanized, transistorized, energized chariot of action that is moving out there in the main stream of society. **Get on the go and talk about Jesus.**

The marvels of up-to-date evangelism by Christians ON THE GO, OUTSIDE THE SANCTUARY, are expressed by Paul who said: "The same Good News that came to you is going out all over the world and changing lives everywhere" Col. 1:6 - LL.

In our march for souls, let us adopt Paul's motto of Christian living: "So everywhere I go, I talk about Christ to all who will listen . . . This is my work, and I can do it only because Christ's mighty energy is at work within me" Col. 1:28-29 - LL.

2
THE CASE IN BRIEF

$\mathcal{H}$ ERE IS THE case for soulwinning — in a nutshell:

1. Sinners do not go to church.
2. Our commission is to reach every sinner ("preach the Gospel to every creature").
3. Inasmuch as sinners do **not** go to church, Christians must therefore go to them, out where they are, OUTSIDE THE SANCTUARY. This is what Christianity is all about. Yet **this** is what most Christians neither understand nor are trained or equipped to do.

It is time to redirect the preacher and the layman to the example of the Early Church where "**daily** in the temple and in every house, they ceased not to teach and preach Jesus Christ" Ac. 5:42.

They did it in the temple — "daily."

They did it in the houses — "daily."

And they evangelized the then-known world.

All over the world, both preachers and laymen **who**

---

care about sinners are discovering new dimensions of ministry. They are finding ways to launch many new outreaches among the UNchurched — OUTSIDE THE SANCTUARY.

The ministry of true **evangelism** belongs to every Christian. It is the ministry of reaching **sinners** with the Gospel. Since they do not go to church, we must go out where the sinners are. This is evangelism!

Many churches have no soulwinning programs outside the walls of their own building.

The Church's principal mission of reaching every sinner is not being carried out because it is not understood and because in the contemporary church it is not **traditional**; and, people usually do only what is traditional — whether it makes sense or not.

But today's world calls for revolutionary changes in church and Christian attitudes toward sinners.

If you think you dare expose yourself to ideas which are not traditional — if you think you are capable of "thinking new" **without** turning to condemn routine concepts; if you think you are big enough to make an honest reappraisal of church and Christian attitudes **about sinners**, and the basic soulwinning concepts of Early Christianity — and most of all, if you think you **actually care about sinners who will not go to church**, then go ahead and expose yourself to these lessons and see what happens. You'll become another of the thousands of rejuvenated Christians ON THE GO, OUTSIDE THE SANCTUARY.

In crusades around the world, Dr. T.L. Osborn has shared God's love with millions face to face.

T. L. OSBORN CRUSADE — ZAIRE

T. L. OSBORN CRUSADE — INDIA

T. L. OSBORN CRUSADE — PUERTO RICO

T. L. OSBORN CRUSADE — HOLLAND

T. L. OSBORN CRUSADE — NIGERIA

T. L. OSBORN CRUSADE — INDONESIA

T. L. OSBORN CRUSADE — PHILIPPINES

T. L. OSBORN CRUSADE — COLUMBIA

T. L. OSBORN CRUSADE — TRINIDAD

Jesus Christ offers God's BEST—faith, hope, love and life to all who believe in Him, as depicted in this masterpiece painting by Gustave Dore (1832-1883).

3
THINK
NEW

WHAT IS THE DIFFERENCE between "Revival" and "Evangelism"? Or did you ever think about it, really? Or does it matter?

I suppose **what we call things** is not so important as **what we do**, yet I believe in the case of Revival versus Evangelism, we would accomplish infinitely more in soulwinning if we clearly distinguished between the two.

"Revival" is **RE**viving something which already had life before. You cannot **RE**vive something that never lived.

But "Evangelism" is giving the Word of Life to those who are **DEAD** in their **trespasses and sins**, who have **never had life** — the UNsaved, the UNchurched. Evangelism is witnessing to and winning souls who are lost.

"Revival" is for **Christians** — for the **church**.

"Evangelism" is for **sinners** — for the **world**.

A sinner cannot be **RE**vived because he is **dead** in

his sins; he has never had Life. So he needs "Evangelism" — he needs to receive the Word of **Life**.

A **Christian** has already received this **Life** from Christ when he believed the Gospel and accepted Christ. But since Christians may become lukewarm or backslidden or lose their first love or become lax in their zeal or vision, they need "Revival"! Therefore:

Inside the sanctuary is the place for "Revival."

Outside the sanctuary is the place for "Evangelism."

The church, among Christians, is where we should conduct **revivals**.

The world, out among sinners, is where we should **evangelize**.

This is a study on "**Evangelism**" or soulwinning — a ministry for **OUTSIDE THE SANCTUARY**.

This fact needs to be clearly understood in order for these lessons to be the help and inspiration for which they are intended.

Read with a willingness to **think new** in order to reach out and to win more souls to Christ.

The preacher or the layman who really cares about the UNchurched masses is willing to revise his thinking and activities in almost any way if it means he and his church can reap a greater harvest of souls.

4

THE NOTORIOUS MENTAL BLOCK

RACTICALLY all functions of church evangelism today are carried on within the framework of a MENTAL BLOCK which assumes the following:

If we can somehow get sinners into our church, then we will get them saved!

So we bring a special speaker to our church. We advertise, inviting people to come to our church, to hear our special speaker.

We invite them by radio, TV and the newspaper.

But, alas, only a few come.

Why? Because **most sinners will not go to church**!

But we can't accept this fact; we love our sanctuary. We have freshly carpeted our aisles and padded our pews. We have a good choir and a fine pastor. Surely sinners will come to this kind of church!

So we bring in the singers, the quartets or the special choir.

Again the faithful ones spread the news and the welcome mat is laid out. More house-to-house calls

are made, inviting people to hear the singers at our fine church. Ads are placed in the papers, on radio and TV.

Again, little results. A few come — some church absentees are recruited, a few dropouts are revived, and a sinner or two attend.

But we invited thousands. Why didn't they come? Our church desires the salvation of souls, and prays for that more than anything else. We have a fine church. Our pastor is one of the best. He has a burden for souls. Our people are concerned for the lost. We have wonderful workers in our congregation — some of the finest counselors and personal workers. Sinners find the most wonderful experiences with God when they come in and are baptized at our church — well that is, the ones who **do** come.

But WHY? Why is it that with all of our efforts to reach people, not many sinners come and get saved?

Because you worked within the traditional church mental block. You were saying to yourselves: "If we can just get sinners to come to our church, we know they will get saved."

And the idea was good — **for those sinners who DID come!**

But the reason more did not come is the simple fact **that sinners do not go to church!**

"Well," we say, "That's a pessimistic view! We don't believe it. Something will surely attract them!"

So we bring the musicians. Again we advertise and promote. Again we call for prayer. Again the church doors swing open. And thank God for those

who **do** come, because even one or two souls are worth **any** investment. But, in general, we do not reach the sinners. Why? We have some of the best musicians available. We lay the groundwork well. Our Christians spare nothing. Yet we fail. In desperation we ask ourselves, "What **will** it take to get sinners into the church nowadays?" And we feel frustrated.

The lost world has been trying to tell us something for a long time:

"Your pastor may have a Th.D., you may air-condition your building, carpet your aisles, cushion your pews, invite us to your church via radio, TV, phone calls, letters, church pages, bulletins, newspaper ads, and personal visits; you may bring preachers, lecturers, prophets, teachers, evangelists, musicians, singers or acrobats, BUT WE STILL WILL NOT COME TO CHURCH!"

Well, then, what are we supposed to do?

Abandon our mental block!

What do I mean by this?

I mean, face the fact that most sinners will never come to church to get saved, and since our commission is to reach sinners with the Gospel, we must, therefore, change our approach and take the Gospel **out where the sinners are** — OUTSIDE THE SANCTUARY — just like the Early Church did.

The only people who can be won to Christ in evangelism are lost sinners, so let's go where they are — OUTSIDE THE SANCTUARY. If we confine our testimony within the sanctuary, the only sinners we can win are those who will deliberately get up, get dressed, travel to the sanctuary and willingly

expose themselves to the Gospel. Most of them will **never** do this.

In the book, "Here's How to Have a Soulwinning Church," the writer says: "The church building is the most evangelized acre on earth. We attempt to evangelize the world by evangelizing the building. We evangelize every classroom and every pew. The way we work at it, you'd think the building itself needed converting. We work as though all the lost people on earth were in the building.

"Only one problem: The lost are everywhere **except** there: The masses of unsaved have never been there, aren't there now, never will be . . . They are everywhere — except where we are trying to win them."

Most Christians today have not realized that there were **no** church buildings in the New Testament. Gene Edwards says: "Today the 'church building' concept of evangelism is the greatest single hindrance to soulwinning. **NOT because we have church buildings — but because we won't get OUT of them!** . . .

"A church building serves one purpose: to keep you from getting cold in winter and hot in summer, or wet when it rains!

"This is not an appeal for you to burn down your church building. Undoubtedly the 'church building concept' is necessary for our day. **But get it in its right perspective!** Realize that evangelism is NOT to be centered in the church building. It is to be centered OUTSIDE THE SANCTUARY. The church is not a place to bring the lost **into**, to convert them. It is a battle station — to send Christians **out** from."

There are **millions** of sinners out there, waiting, needy, desperate, hungry, eager and ripe for harvesting. There they are — right OUTSIDE THE SANCTUARY, in all directions. They need salvation, they want forgiveness, they search for knowledge about Christ, they fear to die as they are, they are encompassed with problems and they yearn for God, but they will not come to church, because they do not know which one they can trust.

But if you go to them, give them the Gospel, **out where they are**, they will accept Christ, and receive His grace and salvation willingly.

Then they will gladly follow you back to your church where they will grow in grace and the knowledge of Christ because they will trust you, your church and your pastor. After all, they know that **you cared for their soul**; you came to them and helped them receive Christ where they were. **They can trust you!** They will go to your church. It cares about sinners!

The most timid Christian on earth who goes to the door of a sinner to witness, says two of the most powerful words in our language before he ever opens his mouth: He says, "I CARE." And human beings want to be loved, to be cared about.

One of the largest chains of American grocery stores experienced their most successful returns by conducting a nationwide promotional campaign with **only two short words**. They said: "WE CARE," then added the small credit line: Safeway Stores, Inc.

The church today must ask herself: Do we really care about sinners — **the ones outside our sanctuary**

— the ones who will not come to our church to get saved?

There is a Southern Baptist Church in New Orleans, La., which has won more people to Christ, on a yearly average, than any other church in that convention. Someone asked that pastor: "Do you do most of your soulwinning by getting people to attend your Sunday School?"

His answer was: "No, we win almost no one to Christ by church enlistment. You see we live in a very **religious** area. The people have strong religious loyalties. **We can get almost no one to 'visit' our church. This is one of the reasons our church is a soulwinning church! We were forced into the position of winning them to Christ in their homes, or where they work. Then after they are really converted and transformed by Christ's New Birth, they come to our church and become strong members.**"

Each year that church receives three or four hundred new converts. And this does not include literally hundreds of others won to Christ by their members, but who join other churches, as well as those who do not join any church.

How does that church do it?

They accept the fact that they cannot wait for people to come to their sanctuary to be converted. Their faithful Christian members **CARE ABOUT SOULS**; they go every week, knocking on doors, house to house. They sit down and preach the Gospel in living rooms, at dining tables, on verandas, at doorsteps, and win souls to Jesus Christ right out there where

the people are so receptive, OUTSIDE THE SANC-TUARY.

And consider the Jehovah's Witnesses. They have been among the fastest growing religious organizations in the Western world. Well, how do they do it?

How many of their converts do they make inside their Kingdom Halls? Practically none! They know that the place to make converts is out in the homes of the people, out where they live and work and play. So they "GO" with their message, and they win millions.

But why haven't we learned by their example?

Because we have inherited a mental block, and we simply have not been able to remove it! Our Sunday School programs, our visitation programs, our Bible Schools, our training courses, almost our entire orientation is designed **to attract sinners into our churches**. THEN we believe we can and will get them saved. But we have the whole thing in reverse — the cart is ahead of the horse.

We have developed and taught and promoted all sorts of programs, ideas, schemes and crusades on **"enlistment** evangelism" — getting unchurched people to attend Sunday School, socials, banquets, singings, classes, studies, festivals, and the church sanctuary. But little or nothing is taught on **how to actually win souls — how to lead men to a decision for Christ** OUTSIDE THE SANCTUARY — at the factory, restaurant, park, on the street, in the sinner's home; and also at the seashore, in

mountain resorts, or anywhere you spend your vacation.

In other words, most churches have excellent programs and training classes on **how to invite men to church** (visitation), but not on **how to get men to accept Christ out where they are** (soulwinning).

In the New Testament, they testified **"house to house"** and made disciples out among the people.

Today the concept is to get men **to church** and **then** to Christ. This system is fine for those who will go to church — but about 90% of the sinners will **never** go, regardless of the attraction.

The New Testament concept is to get men to Christ, THEN to the meeting place — to win them out where they are. This is limitless!

Most training programs are based on recommending the **church or organization**. The New Testament concept was based on recommending **Christ**.

Whether we like to admit it or not, **the church** (as a building or denomination) has the poorest appeal of all to sinners — its rating is exactly ZERO, because **most sinners do not go to church**. Yet the fantastic fact remains that **the person of Jesus Christ** — when He is presented right — has the greatest single appeal to the human heart in this world.

For generations, Christians have been trained, taught, drilled on how to invite people to church, to Sunday School. But now the pendulum is swinging back the other way. Christians are learning to lead souls to Christ — OUTSIDE THE SANCTUARY. They are ON THE GO, talking about Jesus, OUT WHERE IT COUNTS.

This is the Christian ministry which is redis-covered when one truly cares about lost souls.

We must reconsider the very meaning of **"evange-lism"** and see whether or not our church has such a program, and if not, why; and then be willing to do something about it.

Immediately, most people say, "Of course, our church believes in evangelism; certainly we have our evangelistic programs!"

But if your church is not reaching sinners as the Early Church did, then do not be prejudiced against new thinking. Be candid and open-minded and see if a closer look at the Early Church pattern reveals better and more workable concepts for winning lost souls to Christ — **especially those who do not attend the sanctuary**. Then be prepared to GET ON THE GO and TALK ABOUT JESUS out where the sin-ners are. ⌒⤬

"TALKING BOX" shares the big love plan with New Guinea man in his own dialect. T.L. assures him that God is saying, "I love you. I value you. I created you for my BEST."

**20-20
VISION**

*A*CTS 5:42 — "And **daily** in the temple and in every house, they ceased not to teach and preach Jesus Christ."

They did it "daily." They did it in temples, and they did it in **houses**.

Acts 2:46 — "They continued **daily**."

Acts 2:47 — "And the Lord added **daily** such as should be saved."

The Lord can only add "daily" if we evangelize **daily**. Holding services twice a week and having a visitation program to occasionally call on absentees cannot produce a "daily" increase of converts.

If a local group of Christians witnessed "in the temple and in every house" **daily** so that the Lord could add to them "daily," their number would increase by a minimum of 365 per year. I imagine some churches have not attained this **minimum** growth.

Acts 6:7 — "And the **word** of God increased and the number of disciples **multiplied** greatly."

In Acts 2 the Lord was **adding**. But in Acts 6 He was already **multiplying**. Obviously, those Early Christians were getting results.

Acts 20:20 — "I kept back nothing that was profitable unto you and have taught you (1) **publickly** and (2) from **house to house**."

There's the "20-20 Church Vision" — the **public**, pulpit preaching; and the **door-to-door**, house-to-house ministry. Both were carried on **"daily."**

Then, tucked away in Acts 19:10 is perhaps the most fantastic little verse in the Early Church record. Sometimes we come across verses which really test our faith in the Bible. Acts 19:10 is one of them. Is it speaking figuratively? Is it overstated? Can it be taken literally to actually mean what it says?

Acts 19:10 — "And this continued by the space of **twenty years**, so that all they which dwelt in Asia heard the Word of the Lord Jesus, both Jews and Greeks."

Fantastic! Seemingly impossible!

Just 20 years! And "all they that dwelt in Asia" received a Gospel witness.

Just 20 years! Amazing, isn't it?

But did you notice that I MISQUOTED it?

It's not 20 years! It's ONLY **"TWO** years!"

"By the space of **TWO** years, . . . all they which dwelt in Asia" were evangelized.

No radio, television, electricity, tape or record players, loud-speakers, modern jets or even fast ships. No automobiles. Not even bicycles or typewriters.

How then did they do it?

All the Christians shared in the ministry. They

"**ceased not**" witnessing "daily in the **temple** and in every **house**."

They had a 20-20 vision!

They **cared about sinners**!

In TWO years they reached everyone in Asia!

They were ON THE GO, OUTSIDE THE SANC-TUARY.　　　　　　　　　　　　　　　　⊂∞

OSBORN MINISTRIES has provided tons of gospel literature and equipment for Christian workers in Thailand.

THE OSBORNS conduct seminars for Christian workers around the world, like this one in Bangkok, Thailand. (Photos — Top: United in prayer after a teaching session. Bottom: Final day of Seminar. Center and opposite page: Equipped to share God's big love-plan with their nation.)

Over 100 beautiful gospel vans, loaded and equipped with tools for evangelism have been provided FREE for mission fields worldwide, by the Osborn Ministries.

OSBORN CRUSADE —
Bogota

OSBORN CRUSADE —
Accra

OSBORN TEACHING —
Tulsa Campmeeting

OSBORN CRUSADE —
Nigeria

Hundreds of tape players — thousands of gospel tapes

HUGE airlifts of TONS of gospel literature and evangelism tools are provided free to national pastors, leaders and to missionaries overseas, for reaching the unreached with the message of God's love.

OSBORN CRUSADE — ...o

OSBORN CRUSADE — Kinshasa

OSBORN CRUSADE — W. Africa

OSBORN CRUSADE — Calabar

...rovided free by Osborn Ministries.

Miracle films furnished by the Osborn Ministries in 69 languages are showing the gospel in action to millions of souls worldwide.

**CLOSE
THE
CHURCH?**

"WE'RE GOING to begin an **Evangelistic** Crusade," the young pastor announced to his small congregation. "During the crusade, **our church will be closed — except Sundays.**"

What did he mean? How could a local church put on an **Evangelistic** crusade and be closed?

Our traditional pattern is just the opposite: We announce an **Evangelistic** crusade and we all understand that means we'll have meetings in the church every night, that the sanctuary will become the center of the preaching crusade.

But that is what illustrates again our mental block about Evangelism — that we feel we must first get sinners to attend our church, **then** we will get them saved.

The young pastor was 24 years old. He had finished Bible School and was trusting God to lead him into a ripe area for soulwinning.

He went into a large city and found a fine old

church building which had been closed, with boards nailed over the doors and windows.

In 1900, it was the largest church in the city. By 1959 it was deserted and boarded up. For two years there had not been a service in it. The church had died.

Back in 1900, over 800 people worshiped regularly in that fine old church. It was an elite church, in one of the nice residential areas of the city.

Then the wealthy people moved away and poor people settled in the area. In spite of all the denomination could do to keep the church going, the grand old building finally lay empty.

Then in 1959, the young 24-year-old preacher came to town and spotted the church.

Inspired by the opportunity he saw in the area, he found the remaining **seven members** of the old church, met with them, and prevailed upon them to vote him in as their pastor.

Next, he went to a small orphanage nearby and won approval of the manager for the 40 orphans to attend the church on Sunday.

So he began: with 40 orphans, seven members of the old church and his own family (50 in all).

Then he called on a soulwinning evangelist to come and teach his people how to win souls. A unique scene it was: a magnificent old building which would seat 1,000, with ten humble Christians sitting there on the front row — eager to learn how to win souls.

The training course was a success. And it was following that course that the eager young pastor made his unorthodox announcement:

"We're going to begin an **Evangelistic** crusade. During the crusade our church will be **closed** — except Sundays."

Why close the church?

Because they were going **out where the sinners are** to evangelize — OUTSIDE THE SANCTUARY.

Ten Christians had been trained. They were ready for soulwinning action.

Each evening they met for prayer, then each of them was assigned to a different street, and they began a truly biblical **Evangelistic** crusade. They began knocking on doors, witnessing of Christ, house-to-house. (Each Sunday they regrouped with their newly won converts.)

Four Sundays later, they had an attendance of 220! A revival of Early Church **Evangelism** swept that congregation and that was just the beginning.

With no outside evangelist, no extra church expenses, no added heat or air conditioning bills to pay, that church reaped a harvest of souls. They had caught a vision of soulwinning — OUTSIDE THE SANCTUARY. Just 10 Christians went out each evening, visiting homes and winning people to Jesus — out where they live.

But they did not stop in four weeks. They had caught a vision. They were gripped by a fresh, new passion for souls. They made the grand discovery that sinners are easy to win — if you approach them out where they are.

That pastor said: **"Today I have only one problem; my people don't want to do anything but win souls."**

Before the year was out, that church had won more

people to Christ than any other church in that city. They did it OUTSIDE THE SANCTUARY.

* * *

A new soulwinning church was celebrating its **fifth** anniversary. In one year it had reached a membership of 44. Now its attendance was 2,000.

After one year they had still met in a garage, with property worth $6,000 and an annual budget of about the same amount. Now their budget was $200,000 per year and their property was valued at a million dollars.

In the church's five year history, it had **outgrown five buildings**.

Why was this church one of the fastest growing churches in the world?

The pastor explained that he had become pastor of that church when it was only one year old, meeting in a garage. He had announced that whatever else was done, that church **would win souls!**

He trained about ten of his men and started going from door-to-door with them, witnessing to sinners — out where they are — and winning them to Christ.

The first year, they won 150 souls — most of them inside their own homes.

The next year over 300 new converts were brought into the church in the same way.

The next year they won over 500 and the next, over 700.

The pastor said: "Today I have more ushers passing out offering plates than I had members four years ago."

Counting missionaries and their children, that

church was sponsoring 44 people on mission fields — exactly the number they had in attendance four years earlier.

An evangelist questioned that pastor about his amazing success. The pastor said, "Come to our midweek service and I will **show** you the reason for our church's growth."

There on Wednesday evening, over 700 people were in attendance. The pastor asked his congregation, "How many of you have already gone outside our sanctuary this year and won at least one soul to Jesus Christ?"

Over 300 people stood to their feet.

That church had rediscovered the amazing Apostolic soulwinning secret — that if we really care about sinners, and want to win the lost to Christ, anyone can do it if he will just go **out where the sinners are** — OUTSIDE THE SANCTUARY.

* * *

There is a certain pastor who has the distinction and honor of baptizing in water more new converts each year than any other man widely known in the world. His church is among the few most successful soulwinning churches in the world.

An evangelist asked him this question: "Why is it that your church brings more new Christians into its fellowship than almost any other church in the world?"

He answered with only four words: **"My people win souls."**

In four simple words, he had given the key.

That pastor said: "I have emphasized one truth

in my church over and over. I have repeated it until my people have finally come to believe it."

The truth he had so emphasized was:

"And daily in the temple and in **every** house, **they ceased not to teach and preach Jesus Christ**."

That church actually visits in the home of every family that moves into the city. It has five visitation programs per week. It has visited and contacted as many as 10,000 people in one week.

How?

The pastor said he emphasizes soulwinning and Christian witnessing until his people actually believe they should win souls; therefore, they do. He exemplifies it in his own life. He preaches it every time he stands in the pulpit. He never stops emphasizing it. It has taken root in the hearts of his people until soulwinning — outside the sanctuary — has become the one magnificent obsession of that church. Last year they received over 1,400 new converts into their church fellowship.

* * *

But, you say, these are large churches; ours is a small community church.

Sinners live in small communities too. And they are just as responsive to accept Christ, if they are reached with the Gospel **out where they are**.

A certain little church sits out in an open, rural community. Its pastor said, "You can stand on the roof of the church and see only two houses."

When he became pastor, attendance was about 75. (The entire area had no more than 400.)

The pastor took a religious census and found only

six unsaved people in the area — and they were Gospel hardened.

Yet in only two years, that church won over 300 souls to Christ. Their attendance jumped to nearly 400.

How?

The young pastor knew the secret of soulwinning. He knew sinners would not usually come to church to get saved. They had to be reached **outside the sanctuary**.

He trained a group of his people to witness and lead souls to a decision for Christ — **out where they are**. They went all over that area, knocking on doors, presenting Christ to the people, and getting them saved.

They would drive to nearby towns, 15 and 25 miles away, and win people to Christ. In two years that church had three buses picking up some 200 people and bringing them to worship.

* * *

In a district of a large city, a certain church had won 40 people to Christ within a year. They were not satisfied so they put on a two-week soulwinning training course.

The pastor and his congregation set a goal to evangelize **"the world of our community."**

Within just **two months** that church had gone outside their sanctuary and won to Christ scores of people and had brought **67 new families** into their church fellowship.

* * *

A training course on soulwinning was conducted

in another certain church, in a big metropolitan area.

On Sunday night following the session, the pastor had walked into the church and announced that he was dismissing the Sunday evening service. Instead of having a regular church service, he sent his people out to witness. The result was so good that they decided to continue the program for three more nights. The spirit of soulwinning caught fire and a definite program of witnessing from house to house was begun. The church was stunned and grateful at the results.

In a brief period of less than three months, the laymen in the church had gone out and won over 200 souls to Jesus Christ — and the church was on fire.

* * *

In a town of 45,000 people, a church set aside three weeks for an intensive soulwinning campaign — OUTSIDE THE SANCTUARY. The purpose was to **evangelize** their city.

The first week was given entirely to training the Christians on how to witness and lead a soul to accept Christ.

The men witnessed, person to person, in jails, rescue missions, flop houses and in slum areas. The women visited the hospitals, old folks' homes and other convalescent centers, going from bed to bed and chair to chair.

The main thrust of their combined efforts, of course, was in **"house to house" evangelism**. Every evening, the Christians were assigned to different streets. They went into the homes to witness of Christ and to do their best to lead sinners to a decision to

accept Him then and there.

In just **two weeks**, 333 people had actually been led to accept Christ, by actual count, and within the next three weeks, that church received over 150 new converts into its own church fellowship.

That pastor said that his people have become so enthusiastic about **house-to-house evangelism** that their visitation program is large enough to visit every home in the city about every three months.

* * *

A young student on holiday vacation from college attended a church training session on **personal soul-winning outside the sanctuary**. That young man caught the idea.

He returned to college and organized a group of ten fellow students into a soulwinning group called the "Evangelaires," for the purpose of witnessing to sinners.

In **the first month** that group of young students went out and **won over 50 souls to Christ**.

* * *

Another church whose pastor had heard about **soulwinning outside the sanctuary**, requested literature on the subject, to train his people on witnessing to sinners.

They had received only two additions to their church in the past year.

Following their training period, they began to **evangelize — outside their church**, witnessing of Christ from house to house.

Within one year that small church went out and

actually won to Christ **over 100 lost souls** in their own community.

* * *

A Christian professor teaching at Bible College told me of his experience.

He said that he realized that Christians must get out among sinners to witness; that the church could not wait for the lost to come into the sanctuary to be saved. So he decided that he would make a definite test of **soulwinning out where the sinners are**.

He took a group of seven young Christian workers and they went to a certain city.

They devoted three afternoons to house-to-house visitation and witnessing of Christ. They spent two hours per afternoon.

In just three days, two hours per day, they knocked on the doors of 392 houses and were able to talk with 198 people. 24 souls accepted Christ.

* * *

Innumerable examples could be recounted here, and as the secret of soulwinning rapidly spreads among pastors and laymen who care about souls, new examples are being made every week.

There is no question about it: ANY CHURCH CAN WIN SOULS — if the Christians of that church can understand and are willing to be trained and equipped in **Evangelism** (or soulwinning) **out where the sinners are** — OUTSIDE THE SANCTUARY.

THE
GENUINE
ARTICLE

NE OF THE MOST extraordinary 20th Century examples of religious growth is that of the Jehovah's Witness movement.

They have preached and taught their doctrine from house to house, throughout the world. Today they have been reputed to be the fastest-growing religious organization in the Western world.

Yet, I doubt if anyone can ever recall being invited to attend one of their Kingdom Halls on first contact. Their plan is to enter the homes and conduct periodic visits until they have won their converts, **then** those converts are brought to the Kingdom Hall; **but only for the purpose of training them to go out and win others like they themselves were won.**

What inspires these dedicated "Witnesses" to go out and accomplish so successfully what fundamental Christians apparently consider unworkable? And what prevents the fundamental Christians from following their example, now that their method has been

so thoroughly proven? It not only works; it works so extremely well! Won't it work just as well for the church today? It certainly worked for the Early Church. It's rather embarrassing, I think, that the Jehovah's Witnesses have been the ones to prove Early Church methods — so far as **contacting** the unconverted is concerned.

According to the "Witnesses," theirs is a sincere desire to conduct themselves like Early Christians. "Historically," they say, "Christianity is a person-to-person religion." And so they practice talking about their beliefs person-to-person. Is there anything to prevent fundamental Christians from doing the same (apart from fear, indifference, over-involvement in secular affairs, or a misplaced confidence that the job is being done by the overworked professionals "who get paid for it")?

For one thing, the "Witnesses" do not recognize any difference between clergy and laity. "All are preachers and teachers of the Word of God," they declare. Consequently, they do not place the burden of evangelism upon the clerical minority. **Every** Jehovah's Witness is a **witness!**

And, I say, every follower of Jesus is to be a **Jesus-Witness!** If we believe Acts 1:8 for its blessings ("ye shall receive power . . ."), let's also believe its command ("ye shall be witnesses . . .")!

You see, while the Jehovah's Witnesses are spending most of their time ministering in the homes of the public, fundamental Christians are spending their time savoring God's blessings for themselves, inside their sanctuaries.

If the Jehovah's Witnesses had stayed within their Kingdom Halls, probably nobody would have heard any more about them. If the Early Church had stayed in its Upper Room, enjoying the blessings of their new experiences, few may have ever heard the Gospel. But Early Christians went out where the sinners are, and all Asia was evangelized in two years. The Jehovah's Witnesses go out, and when they gather for a convention they pack the largest auditorium or stadium available and spend many hours studying and demonstrating "soulwinning" techniques.

It's time that we take a closer look at their methods, that we get ON THE GO, OUTSIDE THE SANCTUARY.

It seems a shame that while we have what we know to be the Truth, Jehovah's Witnesses, using methods we have ignored or never tried, are claiming that "Through us the Good News is being preached to all the world." They are preaching to every creature what they believe as individuals. May the love of Christ constrain us to preach what we KNOW to sinners in their own homes.

Published figures reveal that 900,000 homes are visited by Jehovah's Witnesses each week. In many of them, they conduct weekly Bible studies. Who of my generation cannot remember as a child being visited by Jehovah's Witnesses with their record or tape-players, to play the messages of the Watchtower?

Today, with sermon tapes and records available, transistorized lightweight tape and record players on hand, and almost unlimited supplies of FREE literature, Christian laymen must recapture this zeal

and passion to take the true Gospel OUTSIDE THE SANCTUARY — out where the sinners are.

After all, we **do** have the Genuine Article: new life in Christ Jesus!

BIRTH
AND
DEATH
OF
EVANGELISM

*L*ET'S TAKE a quick review of Church History and trace the birth of Evangelism, then its disappearance and finally its return to the church.

The Bible says, "Christ Jesus came into the world TO SAVE SINNERS" I Ti. 1:15. That is Evangelism.

<u>Christ</u> is our perfect example.

Early Christians followed His example. They knew their mission was to **win sinners**. They remembered what He said:

"And ye shall receive power, after that the Holy Ghost is come upon you: **and ye shall be WITNESSES unto Me** both in Jerusalem, and in all Judaea, and in Samaria, and unto the uttermost part of the earth" Ac. 1:8.

The Holy Ghost was given to them to empower them to WITNESS, going out and speaking to people house-to-house, person-to-person, with the object of causing them to believe on Jesus Christ and to become His followers.

Their method was simple and practical:

"And **daily** in the temple, and **in every house**, they ceased not to teach and preach Jesus Christ" Ac. 5:42. **"And the number of the disciples** multiplied" Ac. 6:7. That brought on persecution and "they were all scattered abroad" . . . "therefore **they went every where preaching the** Word" Ac. 8:1, 4, **"publickly** and from house to house" Ac. 20:20.

"And this continued by the space of **two years**; so that ALL they which dwelt in Asia heard the word of the Lord Jesus, both Jews and Greeks" Ac. 19:10.

There can be no argument about it: Early Christians followed the example of Jesus. **All of them** were fishers of men. They understood that this was why they were saved, that their purpose was to witness.

What resulted in the Early Church?

They quickly evangelized their world — all of Asia Minor; many large cities like Jerusalem, Damascus, Ephesus, plus innumerable towns and villages. They even evangelized the segregated areas like Samaria, the nomadic tribes in the deserts and the pagan people on the nearby islands. All of this took them only 24 months!

Think of it! Without electricity, radio, TV, tapes, records or films; without loud-speakers, jet airplanes or automobiles; even without bicycles or typewriters. **But they did it** — in just TWO YEARS.

And then they spread out and evangelized North Africa and Southern Europe. They even reached Spain and penetrated the great Northern pagan areas now known as Scandinavia and Great Britain.

Those 1st Century Christians were **witnesses**. They

were **soulwinners**. They won people "publickly" and "house to house" — "DAILY"!

What might have happened if this original zeal and passion for souls had continued in the Church?

But it **didn't**. Instead, in the 2nd Century, Christianity became entangled in theological controversy. Rather than to keep pressing on to the "uttermost part" and to more "regions beyond," they began to argue over doctrinal fine points, and to divide their ranks.

The 3rd Century found the Christians sinking into genuine apostasy.

The 4th Century closed the gap and their backsliding and compromise was complete.

And then Christianity was plunged into 1,000 years of awful spiritual darkness — the Dark Ages, and this terrible thousand years is the veil which has separated the Church of today from the New Testament concept.

This is a synopsis of the origin and subsequent disappearance of Early Church **Evangelism**. Now let's take a look at its return.

Daisy Osborn, called of God to help women discover their position in Christ, reaches out to America in conventions, conferences and special seminars

T.L. TEACHES AT THE COPELAND BELIEVER'S

T.L. Osborn believes Joel's prophecy (2:28-29) is being fulfilled as women rise from traditional silence, and discover themselves in the light of total redemption.

CONVENTION—ATLANTA, GEORGIA

Photo credit: James Overrein

T.L. Osborn joins with Kenneth Copeland to pray for millions of believers worldwide. (Left: Pastor John Osteen of Houston's Lakewood Church; Pat Boone, and Charles Capps.)

BELOW: T.L. and Daisy (opposite page) minister at Lakewood Church, Houston, Texas.

T.L. Osborn is awarded Honorary Doctorate Degree at Oral Roberts University.

Daisy Washburn Osborn is awarded Honorary Doctorates at Zoe College in Florida. . .

. . .and at Bethel Christian College in California.

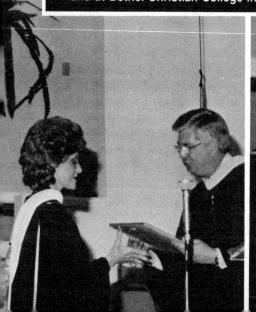

At the Hagin International Campmeeting in Tulsa, Oklahoma, T.L. Osborn, Kenneth Hagin and Oral Roberts unite their faith as they pray for the thousands of men and women consecrating themselves to God's work in this generation.

Dr. T.L. Osborn addresses the graduating body at Christ For The Nations Bible Institute, Dallas, Texas.

SUPERIMPOSED
PHOTOGRAPH

Dr. T.L. Osborn, one of the teachers at the Copeland Believers' Convention, Ft. Worth, Texas, proclaims the value of each human person to God and to His plan, as proven by the price that was paid for our redemption by the death of Jesus Christ.

9
THE
RETURN
OF
SOULWINNING

$\mathcal{M}$ARTIN LUTHER made the first rediscovery of New Testament Christianity with the revelation that "the just shall live by faith."

The Early Church knew this truth but it was lost in the Dark Ages.

But the Reformation of the 16th Century was primarily a theological reformation — a return to examination of the Word of God. It was otherwise very limited, especially in its teachings on mass evangelism, or sanctification, or missions, or the Holy Spirit baptism, or the gifts of the Spirit, or Christ's return, all of which were cardinal truths embraced by the Early Church.

After Luther rediscovered personal faith for each individual believer, Wesley came along in the mid-1700's with the **rediscovery of mass evangelism**, sanctification and the power of the Spirit working in the Christian.

Opposed and rejected by the Orthodox Church,

Wesley rediscovered that you could go out in public fields, parks, or roadways and proclaim the Gospel to the masses where men and women could be saved by the hundreds at one time.

Luther had rediscovered that an **individual** could come directly to Christ for himself, could read the Bible, call on the Lord and be saved THROUGH HIS OWN FAITH. But Wesley rediscovered that a **whole crowd of sinners** could believe on Christ and be saved at the same time.

The Early Church practiced **mass evangelism** but it had been choked to death during the Dark Ages when Christianity was only proclaimed inside the walls of cathedrals and church sanctuaries. But it was rediscovered and has resurged repeatedly under men like Finney, then Moody and again particularly in this century.

William Carey came along about 1790 and rediscovered that the Gospel was **also for the heathen**. So "missions" was rediscovered. The Early Christians were great missionaries but during the Dark Ages the concept of evangelizing far away nations of other colors had disappeared.

Then in the late 1800's and early 1900's, more vital truths were restored to the church: the outpouring of the Spirit, Spiritual gifts, the doctrine of the end time and of Christ's return. Luther mentioned none of these truths, nor did Carey. Even Wesley did not give them prominence.

Across the world, almost simultaneously, Christians began to rediscover the baptism of the Holy Spirit accompanied by supernatural signs. Then the

Gifts of the Spirit began to be exercised, including a rediscovery of Christ's power to heal the sick and the truth of His imminent return.

Early Christians knew all of these vital truths but for a thousand years the church had been out of touch with New Testament concepts. During these thousand years Christians became addicted to religious concepts and attitudes entirely foreign to the New Testament.

If we will remember this 1,000-year veil which obscures our vision of the Early Church, we will be more understanding of many traditions today, rather than critical and judging.

ALL EXCEPT ONE

Since Luther's Reformation, a glorious sequence of revealed truths has unfolded before the church. But the tragedy is that a most vital truth has **not yet** been rediscovered by the institutional church: **That is Personal Soulwinning out among sinners!**

All of the great cardinal truths of Early Christianity have been rediscovered **EXCEPT the motivating truth which moves the church out among sinners, witnessing and winning them for Christ.** Consequently the church is generally closed in behind her sanctuary walls, out of touch with sinners, and her traditional attitude toward those who will not come inside her sanctuary to be saved gives the impression that she could hardly care less about them.

"After all," she seems to say, "Sinners know we

are here. If they want to get saved, let them come to our meetings and hear the Gospel. Here in our sanctuary we will do **anything** to help them find Christ. We love them; we arrange special meetings for them; we constantly pray for them. Here in our sanctuary we are **equipped** to help them: We have our choir, our personal workers, our preachers, our mourners' bench; we are willing to do **anything** in our power, and make any personal sacrifice to help any sinner to find Christ **HERE IN OUR SANC-TUARY.**"

And there is nothing wrong with this attitude EXCEPT that it can only help those who come to the church; it does not express compassion for the 90% of all sinners who will **not** go to church. In other words, it exposes the fact that the rank and file of the church has not rediscovered **Personal Evangelism** — outside the sanctuary — out where the sinners are.

We must understand that the true Church of Jesus Christ today stands **restored to her full stature**, comparable to the New Testament Church **in all except that ONE particular concept** which is actually the key that unlocks the unprecedented success of Early Christianity: **A PASSION FOR PERSONAL WIT-NESSING — PERSONAL EVANGELISM!**

That is why this book is written to urge Christians to "JOIN THIS CHARIOT" . . . to do like Philip; to be ON THE GO FOR SOULS, OUTSIDE THE SANCTUARY, out on the main roadways of life where the rich and the poor, the beggar and the ruler travel together in search of real life. There is where they are. There is where we will find them, and win

them. There is where Christ sends us to "seek and to save that which is lost." There is where His Spirit will speak to us as He spoke to Philip to "go join thyself to this chariot" where we will discover the desperate search of people, for truth, who will never go to church to be saved.

OSBORN MINISTRIES - dedicated to lifting, healing and blessing people around the world: Crusades, Films, Tapes, Literature, Mobile Vans, etc.

A WORLD
OF
SPECTATORS

N "**Christianity Today**," Howard E. Butt, Jr. presented a very strong article about "The Layman as a Witness."

He says, "The Bible stresses that every Christian is a priest. Luther's Reformation doctrine of the **priesthood of every believer** does not mean there are NO MORE PRIESTS. It means that WE ALL ARE PRIESTS OF GOD." Then he points out that in the New Testament the words **kleros** (root of clergy) and **laos** (root of laity) **both refer to the same group of people**. He says that just because a man makes his living at a secular job does not mean that God expects only partial commitment of his life.

Mr. Butt scolds the Church for its erroneous concept of "the clergyman on the front lines, fighting the lonely battle for God, while the members in the rear areas send up supplies so their paid representative can fight harder." He says that it should be "the LAYMAN who is **out on the front lines** (OUTSIDE

THE SANCTUARY) — in his home, office, shop and club. **He is there being God's man.**

"When Jesus said, 'Go ye into all the world and preach the Gospel,' He meant not only Africa, Korea, India, but go ye also into the worlds of business, law, education, mechanics, art, music, government, agriculture."

In other words, go ye into all these worlds and preach the Gospel there — **into the world of your influence, of your acquaintance**, and talk to men about Christ with a view to bringing them to a decision about Him.

Plan on a soulwinning vacation: Visit campgrounds, beaches, health spas, mountain resorts, and any other place that offers opportunities for soulwinning.

"The New Testament Church began with Jesus' command to **everyone of His followers**, the apostles **and ordinary believers alike**: 'Go ye into all the world and preach the Gospel to every creature.'

"But what started as a lay movement has deteriorated into what has been acidly but accurately described as a **professional pulpitism** financed by the lowly laymen."

Mr. Butt says: "Many conceive a ladder of dedication. At the top is the missionary overseas. Just below comes the pastor. Then the professional religious worker. Finally, down on the bottom rung is the lowly layman whose chief function is to pay the bills for the pastor and fill the pews for the public services of the church.

"This is the age of the spectator — the sporting events, where most of us only watch the others perform. Now this spectator concept has spread from the athletic field to engulf the home. Through TV and other mass media, we are a world of **professional watchers**.

"Fred Allen comically predicted that if the trend continues, we may become a race of people whose heads are dominated by huge saucer-sized eyes, our brains having shriveled away to nothing. And since most people watch their entertainment in a sitting position, human beings may become all bottom and no head; just big eyes on top."

An amusing prediction, indeed, but for **watchers instead of participants in the church**, the result may not be so humorous.

Canon Bryan Green of Great Britain predicts the sobering result in America if the contemporary trend in the church is not changed:

"When I was a young man, our English churches were full like your American churches are today. But we were satisfied with big congregations that focused on the pulpit, routine attendance in the pew . . . and our Christian shallowness. Consequently, people became disillusioned by an ineffectual church and indifferent to her message. And today our churches are empty.

"Your American churches are crowded with people today, but there is no biblical or spiritual depth among your laymen. Religion is largely a sentimental Sunday affair which does not radically influence daily life. If something doesn't change, fifty years

from now your churches will be empty as ours are today."

Mr. Butt says: **"We have developed a spectator Christianity in which few speak and many listen.**

"The church was intended to be a vibrant, redeeming community of compassion, mission, service, witness, love and worship — **not a fraternity of fans of the faith!**

"Professional spectators almost always turn into critics, from the sports fan to the theatre-attender to the observer of government who never becomes personally involved but who cynically informs us that all politicians are crooks.

"Spectator-Christianity ultimately becomes critical and contemptuous, cold and cynical, sterile and unproductive. It observes and criticizes others but never gets committed to life with Jesus Christ.

"Theodore Roosevelt described those timid souls who refuse to become involved:

'It is not the critic who counts; not the man who points out how the strong man stumbled, or where the doer of deeds could have done them better.

'The credit belongs to the man who is actually in the arena, whose face is marred by dust and sweat and blood; . . . who errs, and comes short again and again, because there is no effort without error and shortcoming; but . . . if he fails, at least fails while daring greatly, so that his place shall never be with those cold and timid souls who know neither victory nor defeat!'

"The true Christian is involved. He cannot avoid it. He is a **participant** in the redemptive mission of

God, **not a critical onlooker**. He is **involved** in the world — its business, its government, its culture, its hunger, its travail, its tears — **because he loves its people.**

"Jesus said, 'I pray not that Thou shouldest take them out of the world. As Thou has sent Me into the world, even so have I also sent them into the world!' **The layman is sent into the world in exactly the same way Christ was sent** — as an agent of redemption."

Mr. Butt says: "The Christian layman has a life **in the church** for worship, fellowship, instruction, edifying. But from there he moves (OUTSIDE THE SANCTUARY) into the world of unbelief to be a witness, a minister of reconciliation, a servant of God. Christ has reconciled us to Himself by the cross and has committed to us the ministry of reconciliation (2 Cor. 5:14-20). If reconciliation is for all, then obviously the ministry is for **all** as well."

God's love plan is the good news of what Jesus Christ did for each one of us when He died as our substitute, in our name, on the cross.

He assumed the judgment of our sins, to restore us to God as though we had never sinned.

No crime can be punished twice. No debt can be paid twice. He acted on our behalf. We are free.

He arose to restore God's life to us.

11
THE UNRECOVERED TRUTH

 HE SOLE MINISTRY of Early Christians was to **EVANGELIZE!** They understood that the Holy Spirit came into their lives to empower them to WITNESS — everywhere.

Their single passion was to tell people about Jesus Christ and prevail upon each individual to become His follower.

They did this in two ways: **Mass** Evangelism and **Personal** Evangelism.

Mass Evangelism was used as often as possible but it usually attracted city-wide persecution and resulted in the preachers being thrown in jail.

But PERSONAL Evangelism was their KEY!

"Daily in the temple and **in every house**, they ceased not to teach and preach Jesus Christ" Ac. 5:42.

The church today has rediscovered **mass** evangelism but **personal** evangelism has not yet been restored to its rightful place.

Personal evangelism is talked about. People write books about it. Men preach fervent messages about the need of it. And in this generation you are beginning to find people who practice it, but they are the exception — not the rule.

No great, sweeping return to personal evangelism has come to the church. There are encouraging signs, and they are increasing, but not inside the institutional church.

Gene Edwards says, "There has not been a time in the last 1,800 years when a great movement of **personal** witnessing has gripped a large portion of Christian people. Open your history books and turn back through nearly two millenniums. You will discover not even a mention. After 1,800 years, the church has not rediscovered **personal** evangelism.

"The most powerful and necessary concept of Christianity **is still dead**! We have a car without an engine; a plane without wings; a message — **the Message** — and no really effective way to get it out to every creature.

"A rediscovery of **personal** evangelism will, in truth, be the rediscovery of the spirit of New Testament Christianity."

We can be thankful that the seeds of **personal** evangelism, sown through books like this, are beginning to grow and there are worldwide encouraging signs that the concept is getting more consideration everywhere. Indeed, in some areas of the world, revolutionary results are being achieved. But again I emphasize: This is among groups, societies, orders and

associations formed outside the jurisdiction of the institutional church.

Yes, new modern-day Philips are ON THE GO, more and more, and they are **joining the chariots** of men on the move, out where they live and work and play. And multitudes are being reached. May this move toward ACTION OUTSIDE THE SANCTUARY spread to Christians of all the world, until the Gospel is preached to "every creature."

GOD so loved the world that He gave His only Son, that whoever believes in Him will not perish but have eternal life.

SUPERIMPOSED PHOTOGRAPH

THE PRETENDING CHURCH

$\mathcal{T}$HE EARLY CHURCH had no better salvation than believers have today.

The Baptism of the Holy Ghost was no more genuine in Bible days than that experienced by tens of thousands of Christians today.

Their righteousness was no more pure than ours today — through Christ.

Sanctification was no more cleansing then than it is now.

The Gifts of the Spirit were no more real then than today.

Their knowledge of the message of salvation and their practice of miracle healing was no more genuine in the 1st Century than it is in this century.

But those Early Christians **knew what to do with their Spirit-filled lives**, whereas most Christians today have not made that rediscovery.

Consequently, the church today sits comfortably within her sanctuary walls, **pretending** to care about

sinners by praying for them and by inviting them to come into the church to be saved, but actually remaining out of contact with the lost.

Whereas the Early Church was engaged in a continuous house-to-house, market-to-market, person-to-person ministry of **Evangelism**. They knew where the sinners were, and they took the Gospel to them face-to-face. This is what the 20th-Century Church **must** rediscover and put into practice. **She must prove by her actions that she cares about the UNchurched — those who will never enter the sanctuary to be saved.**

As the Church groped her way out of the Dark Ages, rediscovering the basic truths of Early Christianity, she apparently became so absorbed in the spiritual blessings of these revelations that she overlooked the **practical aspect of a Spirit-filled life**. Instead of applying Christianity to the reaching of "every creature," she simply became accustomed to her sanctuary blessings and continued her search for "deeper living" and greater spiritual gifts, rather than going out to win lost souls — out where they are.

It reminds me of nations racing to outer planets when millions here on **this** planet do not have adequate food, clothing or shelter.

The Church races to penetrate the glories of spiritual space, when right OUTSIDE HER SANCTUARY are millions who do not even know how to be saved.

In the race for "spirituality" and the so-called "deeper life," thousands have gone off into extremism and spiritual fanaticism, bringing reproach and em-

barrasment to the Church. I heard of a woman who claims that she has the gift of casting out devils by speaking in tongues. So, as she sits in a congregation, she is seized by this "power", stands up and, in a frenzy, "speaks in tongues" to drive out the devils. She doesn't know who has the devils, but her barrage of "tongues" casts them out — wherever they are.

The Church has become so absorbed in her spiritual blessings that she has failed to rediscover her true ministry to win sinners. Thus, without the objective of witnessing to the lost, she has become so intent on developing her own "deeper life" that spiritual fanaticism and extremism have resulted.

Today, in a quest for spiritual status, the so-called charismatic "glossalalia" has almost become a fad.

If I had only received the **sign** of speaking in other tongues as proof that I was baptized in the Holy Ghost I would be sorely disappointed, because too many people have supposedly spoken in "tongues" who obviously never received what Early Christians received. What I received was **POWER TO WITNESS — out where the sinners are.** Acts 1:8 needs to be very carefully re-evaluated and re-studied today.

What we need is less speaking in "other" tongues and more speaking in our "known" tongue — more **witnessing** — more soulwinning.

But while these contests for deeper living continue with their rallies to exhibit the ever-increasing number of spiritual gifts, a significant rediscovery of **Personal Soulwinning** is being made, which is the KEY

13
CHRISTIANITY
IN
DEPTH

he POWER of the Holy Spirit has been restored to its proper place in the Church during this century. There is no question of the fact that multiplied thousands of true believers are today as filled with the Holy Ghost as Early Christians were — and their baptism is as genuine today as it was then.

Now the church must rediscover the **purpose of this power; that it equips the Christians to go out and witness to men and lead them to Christ.**

But so many congregations have not yet rediscovered that ministry, so they place the premium on "**having the experience**;" then they go to church and exhibit their spirituality to each other, while their minister searches for a **deeper** experience for them to receive.

And this is done because the church has not discovered that **the greatest DEPTH IN SPIRITUALITY is to go out and lead a lost soul to Jesus Christ.**

There was a man who had held the office of Direc-

tor of Evangelism in a large church for 33 years, yet the church was never a soulwinning church. A young minister was called as pastor of this fine old church. He was a zealous soulwinner.

Pondering the problem of this old gentleman who for 33 years had presided over the **evangelism** department without winning souls, he decided on a course of action.

He invited the Evangelism Director to accompany him for a day of house-to-house witnessing. That evening when they returned, several souls had accepted Christ right in their own homes.

Entering the pastor's study, the old churchman fell down at the couch and wept. Turning to the young minister he said: **"Pastor, I have gained a depth in God today that I never knew existed."**

He had helped lead lost souls to Christ.

There is a depth in God to be attained in winning souls to Christ that can never be experienced at the Bible study or the prayer meeting.

Billy Graham says: "The sad fact of the matter is that some of our greatest Bible scholars are our poorest soulwinners."

An evangelist spoke to a men's prayer and Bible study group about going out to witness for Christ from house-to-house.

The leader said, "We can't do that. We're not **deep** enough in God."

The evangelist asked: "How long have you been meeting to study the Bible and pray?"

"Only two years!"

In our Kansas City Crusade, the 17-year-old leader

of a destructive youth gang was converted on Friday night. On Saturday he gave out tracts and got several of his gang to the meeting where they too were saved. On Sunday they all gave out tracts and witnessed and got the rest of the gang saved. On Monday his sister got saved. That gang became a soul-winning gang. It didn't take them two years to be prepared.

When any Christian speaks to a lost soul, prevails on him to accept Christ and places a warm arm around his shoulder or clasps his hand firmly while he leads that soul in the sinner's prayer — whether at a church altar, a park bench, in a house or restaurant or on a street corner, **that Christian is more like Jesus Christ than he can possibly be in any other spiritual exercise!**

Leading a lost soul to accept Jesus Christ is the most **spiritual** experience possible for a Christian! No greater **spiritual** depth can be achieved!

A soulwinner tried to arouse a small congregation to be more evangelistic-minded. The pastor replied: "You don't understand; we don't want a large crowd. We only want to have a small group which can meet together in quietness to study the Word and learn of Christ **in depth**!"

That attitude must change if the Church hopes to win sinners.

Once the premium is placed on **soulwinning**, instead of on the so-called **deeper life**, the church will discover a new **depth** in Christ never experienced by the **"spiritual" recluse inside the sanctuary**.

The world today does not need **deeper** Christians.

It needs Christians who are witnesses and soulwinners. **This IS depth! This is evangelism!**

If the Church expects to impress the world that she really cares about lost sinners who will not come into the sanctuary to be saved, she must learn this secret. And the world **IS** watching for the faintest sign **that Christians care about the lost.**

Dr. Harry Denman, Secretary to the Board of Evangelism of the Methodist Church for 25 years, says: "Unless Christian laymen catch the vision of **personal** soulwinning, the world will be lost!"

Billy Graham says: "The greatest need in the world today is for the preaching of the Gospel to individuals — not by professional clergymen, but by ordinary Christian **laymen!**"

Unless we get the whole church telling the whole Gospel, the whole world will never be **evangelized!**

When Paul spoke about the real Christian, he spoke of a **ministry**: "If any man be in Christ he is a new creature . . . and . . . God . . . both reconciled (him) to Himself by Jesus Christ, and hath given to (him) the ministry of reconciliation" 2 Co. 5:17-18.

"Any man" who is in Christ, is a "new creature" and **he has received a "ministry** of reconciliation." **Every** Christian has **a ministry of reconciling men to God through Christ. That is soulwinning** — regardless of color, race, status or sex! Every hearer is a proclaimer! Every receiver is a sharer! Every Christian is a missionary — an evangelist — a witness! This is **Christianity IN DEPTH!** That is the "deepest" life a Christian can experience. ⌒×

THE
HUMAN
CHANNEL

HEN ANY CHRISTIAN rediscovers the Early Church's vital KEY of Personal Soulwinning, he must remember that this **evangelizing**, soulwinning ministry can be exercised most **effectively** OUTSIDE THE SANCTUARY.

The Church today **must** express its concern for lost souls. It **must** reorientate itself on the purpose of Christianity in this world. It **must prove by its actions** that it CARES ABOUT SINNERS!

The Church is Christ's Body — His voice — His feet and hands. The Church is YOU — individually!

The reason the Gospel has not been preached "to every creature" is because individual Christians have misinterpreted what the Church is. To them it is their denomination, their assembly, their congregation. (And it is correct to speak of the Church as a collective body of Christians.) But from a **personal** standpoint, the Church is YOU! **Your** body is Christ's

Body. He can only witness and minister THROUGH YOU!

The church cannot **send** Christ out, in His Spirit, to bless the poor, comfort the distressed, visit the sick and convict the sinners.

Christ has sent His Spirit into YOU. YOU are the church. So the only way Christ can visit the sick and witness to sinners is through His Body. That is **YOU!**

Christ's ministry in your community is limited to YOU! He longs to speak to souls about salvation, to convict them of their sins and convince them of the Gospel — this is the work of the Holy Spirit — but HE IS IN YOU, regardless of your sex; He speaks through YOUR lips. If YOU don't go and witness or speak the message, YOUR community will be lost. Christ desires to live IN YOU and He cannot visit the lost independent of YOU, no more than He can stand in the public place and preach the Gospel without a preacher to preach through.

We love to pray and send up a barrage of nice little errands which the wonderful Holy Spirit can just "move" around and carry out for us. It saves **us** the trouble. Besides we are so busy — with our TV programs, our clubs, our recreational activities, and our own private concerns.

No wonder the unconverted throngs mock the Church and the Christians!

No wonder the Marxists ridicule Christianity!

This is one reason the Jews reject Christianity. Their leaders read the New Testament. They know who Jesus was. They know He was a Jew. They know how He lived. And they know how He told His fol-

lowers to live — and they know how differently Christians live today by comparison.

Jesus was a soulwinner. Jesus mixed with people. He befriended the needy. He healed the sick. He spoke the Good News to sinners. He helped people — unselfishly — all the time.

HE HAS NEVER CHANGED! He wills to do the same today! "He works IN YOU both to **will** and to **do** His good pleasure."

THIS IS CHRISTIANITY **in depth**! Everything else is artificial and shallow. Christ is in YOU. You now have purpose in living and witnessing. You have been filled with His Spirit for a **reason**; not just to go to church and to be "spiritual," but to go OUTSIDE THE SANCTUARY and tell men about Christ.

Let us remember that the Holy Spirit operates **through US**. WE are His Temple. If we are too busy to witness, He has no other channel to minister through. He lives in OUR bodies.

Sinners in your community will never be visited by our Lord, if YOU do not go and speak in His Name.

Those who are sick and in prison shall never be visited by the Holy Spirit if YOU do not go to them in His Name.

Men shall never see God — except as they see Him in YOU!

Christ's love can only be manifested through YOUR life. His compassion and concern for lost souls can only be exhibited through YOU.

Jesus Christ visits sinners in your community **only** when YOU do.

That is why, to **EVANGELIZE**, Christians must go OUTSIDE THE SANCTUARY. That is where the sinners are. And that is the chief ministry of **Christians**, to reach sinners with the claims of the Gospel. That is **Evangelism**! He commands us to reach "every creature." This can only be done OUTSIDE THE SANCTUARY.

"Revival" is for inside the sanctuary. But "Evangelism" **at its best**, must be out where the sinners are. That is why Christians must be ON THE GO, OUTSIDE THE SANCTUARY.

Christians need occasional "Revival". This book preached and taught to Christians in the sanctuary or classroom will produce a "Revival" of soulwinning — of concern and compassion for the unsaved, unchurched masses.

But when that "Revival" comes, then we shall "Evangelize" — we will launch exciting, new outreaches to win lost souls. We will do this OUTSIDE THE SANCTUARY. **That** is what this book is about.

This is what God was saying to every Christian when He told Philip to "JOIN THIS CHARIOT." He was saying: Get out there on the busy thoroughfare of life, out there where the world is on the move, and find someone who is lost, and witness to them and win them to Christ.

As long as you confine your testimony within the walls of your church building, God will never be able to guide you to the chariot where a soul is seeking salvation.

But get outside — out where the sinners are — out ON THE GO, out among the traffic and din of hu-

manity, out in public places, and the Holy Spirit will guide you to the very chariot where you, too, will lead souls to Christ.

This is the ministry of **every** Christian, regardless of sex or age, regardless of race, or background; it is the ministry for every man, woman, boy and girl who has received Christ.

OSBORN CRUSADE—Enugu

VISITATION
OR
SOULWINNING

*I*T IS IMPORTANT that we distinguish between a **visitation** program, and **soulwinning**.

The church has recovered the major, basic doctrines of Early Christianity, but not since before the Dark Ages has personal soulwinning out among sinners been her passion.

A revival of this truth is imminent, if for no other reason than that this is the kind of church that was born at Pentecost and, therefore, this is the kind of church which Christ will return to receive unto Himself.

There is evidence that the truth of personal evangelism is breaking out of its shell to come forth in full life and vigor. Everywhere, alert preachers and dedicated Christians are discussing it. Writers are dealing with it. Preachers are talking about it. New programs are being inaugurated.

But most approaches, thus far, have stopped short. The contemporary trend is "visitation." Some

---

call it "enlistment" evangelism. There are many versions and schemes, but most of them stop short of soulwinning — outside the sanctuary. These numerous plans of "visitation" or "enlistment" evangelism have become the most carefully planned programs of the church. More books have been written and more programs worked out in this field than all other forms of evangelism.

And it is fair to say that these forms of evangelism are responsible for more conversions than everything else we do in evangelism combined, though they usually limit the results to those sinners who will come to church, which is about 10% of them. What ought we to do about the other 90% who will not come to church?

The ideas put forth in most circles do not consider this 90%. The usual concept is to go out and contact people and invite them to church, to a program, or a banquet, or a class, a club, a special meeting or whatever we can think of, to get people to come to church.

We assume that getting people **saved** is a highly technical art, reserved for the pastor or professional worker at the church. Since it is usually assumed that ordinary laymen are not capable of actually getting souls saved, they are only supposed to go out and enlist people to attend church. **There is the church building**, the pastor will get them properly saved.

These programs are good, but they fail to recognize the imposing fact that 90% of the unconverted will never come to the sanctuary.

This fact MUST be reckoned with!

A young Christian in England was inspired by one of our Soulwinning lectures. She went out and began witnessing among non-conformist youth groups and within a few days, had won a group of them to Christ.

She asked a pastor if she might bring her new converts to church. But she failed to explain that their clothes and hair might not conform to traditional standards.

Upon entering the church with her group, she was sharply reprimanded for having brought such worldly and inappropriate people into the sanctuary. They were directed to return only when their hair and dress styles conformed to "church" standards, and the young leader was told: "Your place is in church, yourself, where you can learn how to be a Christian. You have no business going out making nonsense of a Gospel testimony. You must leave the work of witnessing to us who are authorized to do so."

But this young Christian had done exactly what the woman of Samaria did after she believed on Christ. Few "professionals" have ever been able to witness with the success of an ordinary Jesus-person. The world does not want the counsel of a religious professional; they want to know about Jesus Christ, in the simplest terms possible — terms which they can relate to without complication.

Christian laymen must be inspired and taught to go into the homes of sinners and lead them to decisions for Christ right there where they witness to them.

One can go to any Bible book store and secure nu-

merous "visitation" plans, well prepared and very good — so far as they go.

For a hundred years, an increasing number of plans have been published. In the last twenty years, they have mushroomed. More and more Christians are visiting sinners in their homes — and this is good. It is one step closer to the real heart of Christianity, and I am encouraged to see the increase of these plans.

But in most churches where these plans are in use, laymen are NOT encouraged to go out and bring sinners **to a decision** about Christ. It is felt that this should be done at the church; that laymen should only enlist the contacts.

But the fact that 90% of the unconverted will NOT go to church, indicates clearly that laymen must be prepared to go outside the sanctuary and win sinners there where they witness to them.

Suppose a vacuum cleaner company would send well-groomed, polite representatives through the community to knock on doors and introduce themselves:

"We're from the Gobbledust Vacuum Company. We'd like to invite you and your family to a special meeting at our lovely new showroom. We have a fine program arranged, with the choir from the Vacuum Cleaner Salesmen's College. Our District Sales Manager will be speaking. He's an excellent speaker and you'll love him."

The strategy would be: if we can just get them into our sales meeting, we'll sell them a vacuum cleaner.

There's nothing wrong with this idea and every

sale made this way would help the company. The only problem is that the company would most likely go broke — not because their vacuum cleaners were not good, but because their sales would be limited to the small percent of prospective buyers who would actually get dressed and drive across town to attend the meeting.

And this is precisely why vacuum cleaner companies do not operate that way. They train their representatives thoroughly, and send them, with their product, out into the homes and make their sales there on the spot.

No wonder Jesus said: "The children of this world are in their generation wiser than the children of light" Lu. 16:8.

The **nature** of the Early Church was to witness to men and win them to Christ, wherever they found them. This is natural to a real Christian — until he learns, from tradition, to leave soulwinning to the preachers and professional workers.

The owner of a large hotel in Holland was converted in our great crusade there. For days, thereafter, he was heard witnessing to his guests and urging them to believe on Christ.

It is **natural** for a new convert to want others to receive this salvation. The church should encourage this. But she usually only advocates what contemporary tradition allows.

The general concept is that Christians are not qualified to deal with sinners. It is felt that they may be confronted with arguments or resistance with which they cannot cope.

That's why we should TEACH soulwinning!

Usually, churches do not elect novices to teach Bible classes. Successful churches hold regular teachers' training classes to cultivate and prepare members for teaching.

In the same way, churches must conduct regular and systematic soulwinning classes, to cultivate and train and promote this greatest ministry on earth for Christian laymen.

Companies train their salesmen.

Jehovah's Witnesses train their members.

Churches train their teachers. Classes and conferences are conducted to train people in "visitation" programs.

But almost no church trains its members in the **art of soulwinning**. You can scarcely find a Bible School or seminary where the curriculum includes courses to promote soulwinning and to train students in this ministry outside the sanctuary. Yet it is the glorious truth — the golden key — to the success of the Early Church.

With all the major, basic truths of Early Church doctrine recovered today, the time is at hand to rediscover **what to do with all of this truth**; we must go out and share it with sinners!

Once this truth regains its proper place in Christianity, the Bible will become a fresh, new book to the Church. Writers will produce volumes of glorious and inspiring truths about soulwinning. Thorough courses will be designed, conferences will be held, classes will be scheduled and pastors will discover unlimited sources of fresh inspiration for teaching

their congregations, both men and women, how to go out to witness and to win lost souls, like Early Christians did — OUTSIDE THE SANCTUARY.

Teachers of soulwinning will be in demand. Both men and women will find a new dimension of ministry. Evangelists will teach witnessing as part of their ministry. Youth groups will find new purpose in Christianity. Dormant congregations will come to life. A whole new era of renewed Christianity will command the stage of action once again. The church will be persecuted again but she will become a moving force in her community for good.

There is a genuine stirring among devoted believers everywhere. They say, "We are not content to sit in our comfortable churches. We feel something is missing. We have a fine pastor and a lovely building. But somehow we are not satisfied. We're not winning sinners. We have a fine "visitation" program, but sinners do not attend our meetings.

This is the Spirit of God, seeking to stir His people into soulwinning action — outside the sanctuary.

"Visitation" is church members going out inviting people to some phase or activity of the church. **But "Personal soulwinning" is one person talking to another person about his need of Jesus Christ as his only Savior, with the view of bringing him to a decision right then and there. THIS IS THE MINISTRY OF EVERY BELIEVER OF BOTH SEXES**.

We certainly do not discourage "visitation." It has been a strong arm of church evangelism. I wish to repeat again: We ought to get every sinner possible

to come to church and we ought to get them saved when they do come.

But we ought not to CONFINE our soulwinning to the church building.

We ought to inaugurate new plans and schemes, and training courses, and programs of PERSONAL EVANGELISM, teaching Christians how to actually lead a lost soul to accept Christ and to be born again. The men ought to do it. The women ought to do it.

We ought to prove to the 90% of the UNchurched that we care about them too — that our Christ will save a wretched sinner right in his own house, or at the factory, or in a park just as gloriously and genuinely as He will save him at a sanctified church altar.

Get outside the sanctuary with your Christian witness, out on the boulevards of life where the world is moving, and the Holy Spirit will show — as He showed Philip — which souls to speak to and YOU will become a WINNER OF SOULS — not just a visitor.

16
WOMEN
IN
REDEMPTION

*T*HE OBJECT of this chapter is to help women find their rightful place in God's work, so they can be active in soulwinning ministries for His glory.

"And it shall come to pass afterward, that I will pour out My spirit upon all flesh; and your sons and your daughters shall prophesy, your old men shall dream dreams, your young men shall see visions:

"And also upon the servants and upon the handmaidens in those days will I pour out My Spirit . . . And it shall come to pass, that whosoever shall call upon the Name of the Lord shall be delivered" Joel 2:28-32.

Let's go back to the beginning of time and look at the creation of woman: "So God created man in His own image, in the image of God created He him; male and female created He them" Gen. 1:27.

"And the Lord God said, It is not good that man

should be alone; I will make him an help meet for him" Gen. 2:18.

It is interesting that God said to man, at his beginning, "It is not good for you to be single."

Apparently, it was never His design that a man should live alone. From the dawn of human history, God's design for man included a woman at his side; that they share with each other, work and live together, love and play together, side by side — **one unit** under God.

That is companionship. It implies co-operation, working side by side, worshipping and praying together, serving together, ministering together, winning souls together.

"I will make him an help meet."

Let Christian men learn that their wives are their "help meets" in life — not their slaves or servants, but their partners, sharers, companions.

"And the Lord God caused a deep sleep to fall upon Adam, and he slept: and He took one of his ribs, and closed up the flesh instead thereof.

"And the rib, which the Lord God had taken from man, made he a woman, and brought her unto the man. And Adam said, This is bone of my bones, and flesh of my flesh" v. 21-22. That is the way a man should feel about his wife; He should love her as his own flesh (Eph. 5:28-29).

"Adam said . . . She shall be called Woman, because, she was taken out of the Man. Therefore shall a man leave his father and his mother, and shall cleave unto his wife: and they shall be **one** flesh" v. 23-24.

That is God's will for man and woman! It is a glorious, loving companionship. Marriage is the happy state of one man and one woman, sharing life together in love. That was the way God intended for it to be.

Adam and Eve were contented. They loved each other. They were **one** flesh. But then, that first man and that first woman disobeyed God, and their sin brought upon them the penalty of His law. They were driven from the garden of Eden, because they could not live in God's presence after they had sinned. They became the slaves of Satan whom they had obeyed. Thus, they had a new master, and that is where the trouble began.

In the heart of man and woman, lust began to take the place of love. Greed and evil took the place of good. Passions were unleashed. And because man had a larger physique and stronger muscles, the evil in his heart made him turn the woman into his slave. Instead of a loving help meet and companion to protect and care for, he reduced her to an inferior physical medium for the satisfaction of his own lust.

But like all of the evil consequences of sin, thank God a remedy has been provided for this fallen state of the woman — a redemption through which she has been restored to her rightful place at man's side. That remedy was in the death and sacrifice of Jesus Christ our Lord, Who came to suffer the consequences of **all** of our sins — those of women as well as those of men. He came to ransom all of us back to our position with God and with each other.

While it is true that the woman, Eve, yielded to the temptation of sin first, and then tempted her husband, let us not forget that it was a **woman,** Mary, who was the obedient vessel through which Christ was conceived of the Holy Spirit, and through whom the Savior of the world was born. So if we blame a woman, Eve, for the fall of man, let us hail a woman, Mary, for being the vessel through which man received the Savior.

In the Bible, both men and women followed Christ. Women were blessed, forgiven and healed the same as men.

A woman who had five husbands, and who was living with another man (to whom she was not married), was blessed and forgiven of all her sins. As proof that Jesus never held the sins of this woman against her, the very day she was converted, she became one of His evangelists (Jn. 4:28-29, 39).

Jesus included women when He said to **all** believers, "He that believeth on Me, the works that I do shall he do also" Jn. 14:12.

It was a woman who preached the first sermon on the resurrection. And she preached it to the **apostles themselves.** Jesus told her to do it! (Jn. 20:17-18).

Today, women are often told not to preach or teach, yet Jesus sent a woman to "Go tell My brothers, that I am risen."

Where were those brave men on the morning that Jesus rose from the dead?

A **woman** was there!

It appears that the men were discouraged after the

unexpected reproach of the crucifixion, and according to John 21:3, they returned to their fishing nets; but the *women* went to the tomb. They were there the morning Christ arose from the dead!

The resurrected Christ appeared and spoke first to a **woman!**

It is strange that the women are told to be quiet today, that they may not preach or teach the Gospel. **The fact that Jesus sent a woman to deliver the first news of His resurrection may be a clue that His death and resurrection lifted woman from her fallen state and restored her to her rightful place in His Kingdom, alongside her husband — equally worthy to give out the New Testament message of Christ to all the world.**

Jesus specifically included the women when He said that they would receive power, when the Holy Ghost was come upon them. And for what purpose? **To be His witnesses.** If the women were not to be flaming WITNESSES of Christ's resurrection, as well as the men, then why should they have been specifically mentioned in the account?

"These all continued with one accord, in prayer and supplication, **with the women"** Acts 1:14.

"And they were **all** filled with the Holy Ghost" Ac. 2:4 — (with the women). And what was the Holy Spirit given to them for? "You shall receive power . . . **to be My witness,"** Jesus said (Ac. 1:8). That means to preach, to teach, to demonstrate, to work miracles, to give proof of His resurrection.

Never forget: the women were there on the Day of Pentecost. The women received the Holy Spirit

as well as the men. "They were **all** filled."

But what for?

Were the **men** filled with the Spirit so that they could go out and preach the Gospel with power, while the **women** were filled with the same Spirit so that they could remain silent?

No, they were **all** filled with the Holy Ghost so that they could ALL be **proof producers of the resurrection!**

When you understand how the women were treated before Christ came to restore them to their original and rightful place alongside the men, you're going to marvel that the Holy Spirit specified that the women were there **with the men** when the power of God came upon His people.

This experience electrified the community. Crowds assembled to witness this strange but marvelous event. People from all the nations were gathered in Jerusalem at this important time. What they saw, astounded them. And I think one of the things that shocked them was that the women were in the midst of it all.

So Peter stood up to explain what was happening. He knew it was the divine fulfillment of a major prophesy. Both the men and the women were affected.

Peter said, "Look, we're not drunk as some of you suppose; this is the fulfillment of Joel's prophesy, 'I'll pour out My Spirit upon **all** flesh: Your sons and **your daughters** shall prophesy' " Ac. 2:15-17.

He said, in essence: "You Jews never allowed the women to enter the 'House of God', and you marvel that the women are here with us, receiving the same power as the men. But you Jews have forgotten that one of your own prophets, by the name of Joel, said that this would come to pass.

"Joel predicted that in the **last days,** God would pour out His spirit upon ALL flesh. In the **last days** His sons and **daughters** would prophesy."

Yes, after Jesus paid for the sins of every man and **every woman,** then He restored them both to their position with God. The women regained their place in God's plan, to be His instruments, the same as the men. This position was never restored until after Jesus had died for the sins of every man and every woman. **At Calvary, female slavery was abolished forever!**

But it has been almost 2,000 years since Jesus liberated women, and yet today, church tradition often forbids women to preach or to teach. This restriction is based on a few remarks made by Paul which, we shall show in the next chapter, are as inapplicable today as it would be to require all church members to sell their possessions because they did it in Acts 4:34.

Theologians have not emphasized the fact that Christ's redemption restored woman to her original place by man's side. So they often forbid women to speak, to teach, or to preach in the church.

The following chapter will help you understand the circumstances in which Paul made his two statements about women, then you will understand why he made them. ✄

Daisy Washburn Osborn shares her faith worldwide. Some of her dynamic messages: *WHEN WOMEN BECOME WINNERS, GOD'S WOMAN, THE NEW WOMAN FOR THE NEW CHURCH*, etc.

THE
WOMEN
TOO

$\mathcal{T}$HE MINISTRY of winning souls and of witnessing for Christ, outside the sanctuary, is for **the women too**.

This chapter is included because women constitute an enormous army of soulwinners to share the Christ-commissioned ministry of Evangelism.

In many church organizations, women are forbidden to speak or teach, due to the interpretation of certain statements made by Paul, whose remarks were prompted by circumstances entirely foreign to churches in our generation.

The old Jewish temples emphasized class distinctions in their religions. There were six separate courts: 1) The Court of Gentiles for foreigners, on the outside; 2) the Sacred Enclosure where no Gentile could enter without death; 3) the restricted **Court of Women**; 4) the Court of Israel for male Jews; 5) the Court restricted to Priests; and 6) the House of God.

But in the redemptive work of Christ, all of those

---

partitions were broken down and every believer, regardless of race, sex or other distinction, stands on equal ground before God.

The new Christian Dispensation ushered in a new era. In Christ, all divisions were obliterated between Jews and Gentiles (Ro. 10:12), between men and women (Gal. 3:28), and between priests and laymen (Re. 1:6).

But it was not easy for those early Christians to accept this new spiritual equality for women. The idea of them taking part in religious ceremony was so remote as to be downright sacrilegious. They were not even allowed near the court of worship.

Those Jews who had been converted to Christ clung to many old customs. Some refused certain meats. Others continued the practice of circumcision. Much disagreement was caused by those who could not give up the letter of the law, and the matter of women being allowed in the church was certainly not least of their annoyances.

Their seating arrangement in their meeting places was a direct hangover from the Jewish Temples. There had always been a restricted Women's Court, so the women were limited to the rear sections where their gossip and babbling would not disturb the sacred worship. The **men** who had always been the holy instruments of God, occupied the principal section where they could exercise spiritual worship, conduct their meetings, debate and discuss current issues, business affairs and problems, and officiate in their ceremonies. (Churches in some countries still seat the women separately.)

As far as the women were concerned, in Paul's day, they were generally regarded as little more than human chattel; usually uneducated, uncultured and unsophisticated.

In the new Christian revolution, male Jews who were converted, grudgingly conceded the fact that women could be saved. But considering their prejudices against lowly females, it was mental agony to integrate them into the sanctuary, and it was out of the question for these "inferior creatures" to speak or teach. Male superiority could not tolerate that degree of indignity.

The woman's new found liberty in Christ was in direct conflict with the old Jewish system, and the result was the hangover of a distinct male/female barrier among those early Christians.

To make matters worse, the women were not usually educated and they tended to flaunt their new freedom like any suppressed people who are suddenly emancipated. They had always been kept out in the Women's Court. Now, they could come inside the building where they could see and hear everything.

This was intriguing. It fired their spirits. Some were outspoken; others were boisterous and clamorous; others were insatiably curious and inquisitive. This was a new dimension. But their presence and palaver was an offense to men already strained to the limit by this new liberty that allowed females inside the house of worship.

When these women overheard discussions in the church, some of them could not resist yelling at their husbands, asking for explanations; or one might ob-

ject to an issue, or enter into the discussion, or propose a question, or even give a prophecy or an interpretation — and usually in a disorderly manner, calling from the women's section, clamoring to be heard by the men.

Remember, this agitation was the expression of **the world's first emancipated women**. They were not trained or disciplined in their new role of freedom in Christ. To sit inside the church and to hear and see everything for the first time, was an overwhelming experience. They had not learned to restrain themselves, so they blurted out whatever they thought or felt.

Paul was trying to establish some order and dignity in this new Christian freedom. It seemed entirely inappropriate to him for those women to flaunt their new freedom and yell out from the rear "Women's Court," asking questions, or asserting their new freedom by giving prophecies or arguing doctrine and trying to teach the men ideas which they felt had been revealed to them. With children crying and women clamoring for the attention of the men, it was a shameful display, an embarrassment to those newly converted Jewish males. Paul knew something had to be done. Those women were exploiting their new liberty, and they had to learn to cope with their new emancipated role in Christ.

This is the context in which Paul counseled:

"God is not the author of confusion, but of peace, as in all churches of the saints. Let your women keep silence in the churches; for it is not permitted unto them to speak; but they are commanded to be under

obedience, as also saith the law.

"And if they will learn anything, let them ask their husbands at home; for it is a shame for women to speak in the church" — or as one might paraphrase that last line: for it is uncomely and inappropriate to hear them calling out to their men, from the rear "Women's Court;" it is not in good taste for them to yell out for explanations or comments; let them wait and discuss the matters with their husbands at home. 1 Co. 14:33-35.

This is why Paul said, in 1 Ti. 2:11, "Let the women learn in silence with all subjection, But I suffer not a woman to teach, nor to usurp authority over the man." It was not gracious or suitable for those energetic and unrefined women to stand up and disturb the assembly. Some of them were impulsive enough, in their unconventional state, to take issue with the men publicly, to argue or persuade public opinion by teaching their point openly.

Imagine the turmoil and agitation a strongwilled village woman could cause in a situation like that. No wonder Paul said, "I will not suffer that." "Let them learn in silence," and if they have questions, "ask their husbands at home."

I can understand this because I have been in many countries where women are still shackled by tribal customs, bought and sold like animals, owned and used by men. In many areas, women are forbidden to participate in heathen rites or to attend a sacrifice. They are oppressed and have no free expression.

In many countries today, when those people are converted and when those women discover their new

freedom in Christ, it takes time for them to adjust to their new role as a free Christian woman.

In underdeveloped areas, I have seen the same confusion that Paul experienced. I've had to tell rowdy, uneducated village women to be quiet, to wait until they were home to discuss the matter. It was inappropriate for bare-bosomed women to stand up and argue a point with a nursing baby hanging to a breast while they gestured in unsophisticated market-style.

In some Moslem areas where women are veiled because of the disgrace to them for any man, except their husband, to look upon their naked face, they are ill-at-ease in public. Ofttimes I have told Moslem men to bring their wives, which is a strange experience for those women. I've seen them get so excited about the Gospel message that they would disturb our meetings by loud discussions, spontaneously yelling out questions to their husbands, asking for explanations about what I had said. This is the situation Paul confronted, and it is as inapplicable in today's modern society as a horse and buggy on a busy turnpike.

To tell sophisticated, educated, modern Christian women that they must be silent in evangelism is archaic. There is not another single element of today's society that imposes such a primitive tradition on modern people. And the loss to the Church in converts is no longer tolerable. Time is running out. The Church must unshackle this formidable army of woman-power and organize it into evangelism outreaches that can win MILLIONS EXTRA.

In modern society, women are as educated as men.

Our cultures are refined. Public religious services are no longer an open forum of babble and discussion. They are usually organized and orderly, and our seating arrangement is no longer a hangover from the Old Testament. Besides, Paul said: "We are no longer Jews or Greeks or slaves or free men **or even men or women**, but we are **all the same** — WE ARE CHRISTIANS; we are **one** in Christ Jesus" Gal. 3:28 - LL.

Today, in this century, we are no longer in the Dark Ages. Women are as effective in business, science and education as men. Several nations are governed by women. Some of the largest business institutions on earth are presided over by women.

It is archaic to relegate women to silence in God's work because of a couple of statements made by Paul which were entirely valid in his circumstances, (and are valid today in pagan villages among newly converted village women), but which are **inapplicable** to modern society and custom. It is like requiring Christians to bathe the feet of a visitor because it was the custom in Bible days. When a traveler arrives in an air-conditioned car, wearing form-fitted shoes, his feet hardly need bathing. But for the ancient visitor, who had trodden many miles over hot, rough trails, wearing crude sandals, nothing relieved his weariness like a cool cup of water and a bath for his tired feet.

God's Word makes it clear that He ordained men to head the home, women to be subject to their husbands in the Lord; that men should love their wives as their own flesh and that women were created for the men and not vice versa. But these cardinal facts were

never intended to silence the women in evangelism nor to shackle their anointed ministry of winning souls.

In order to "rightly divide the Word of God", we cannot single out two statements by Paul which were made within the context of a totally different social system, and set aside all of the other hundreds of Scriptures about women — as well as common logic itself.

Women had a great and significant share in God's work throughout the Bible, in spite of being bought and sold like human chattel, restricted from the place of worship, and generally deprived of education. Even against such imposing barriers, many of them rose against formidable obstacles to take their places in history among the giants of all times. Miriam, Deborah, Huldah, Noadiah, Anna; Philip's daughters; Athaliah, Esther and the Queen of Sheba, not to mention many other names like Ruth or Hannah or Abigail, are prevalent throughout the Bible.

The last person at the cross was a woman (Mk. 15:47).

The first person at the tomb was a woman (Jn. 20:1).

The first person to proclaim the message of the resurrection was a woman (Mt. 28:8).

The first preacher to the Jews was a woman (Lk. 2:37, 38).

Among those who attended the first prayer meeting were women (Ac. 1:14).

Among the first to be endued with the power of the Holy Spirit, in order to become witnesses for Christ,

were women (Ac. 2:4; 1:8).

The first persons to greet the Christian missionaries in Europe — Paul and Silas — were women (Ac. 16:13).

The first European convert was a woman (Ac. 16:14).

This book deals with the ministry of Christians OUTSIDE THE SANCTUARY. It should be a comfort to women that the only area where they have ever been forbidden to speak is "in the churches" — that is, inside the buildings. (The Greek word which Paul used means particularly "a religious congregation," "assembly," "Jewish **synagogue**."

So, even if the primitive muzzle must be kept on modern Christian women "in the churches," there is no traditional or Scriptural restraint on the ministry of Christian women OUTSIDE THE SANCTUARY, and **that is where the ministry of soulwinning is most effective anyway**.

Mrs. Osborn has always said: "Why should the women feel limited in their ministry just because they are muffled inside the church?

"The Christian message and testimony and ministry of women is needed a million times more outside the sanctuary than inside.

"The whole world is our field.

"We should not feel deprived when we are not allowed to speak **inside** the church. Our ministry and our message count most OUT WHERE THE SINNERS ARE.

"So, rather than complain about the little corners where we are restricted, let us, as women, lift up our

eyes and look on the fields of the WHOLE WORLD, where neither tradition nor Paul's restrictions apply any limits to our ministry, whatsoever.

"If we feel obliged to obey Paul **'inside the sanctuary,'** should we not feel equally obliged to obey our Lord Jesus Christ **'outside** the sanctuary'? Should we give greater obedience to Paul than to Christ?"

When Jesus commanded: "Go ye into all the world and preach the Gospel to every creature," that commission was for every believer, regardless of sex, color, race or culture.

When He categorized the miracle signs that would accompany the ministry of evangelism, he specified "These signs shall follow THEM THAT BELIEVE." That included both sexes.

Jesus said: **"He that believeth on Me,** the works that I do shall he do also." That included both men and women, and many great women leaders have been strong and courageous enough to prove it. John 14:12-14 is for both sexes. It includes women, IF WOMEN HAVE ENOUGH FAITH TO BELIEVE IT AND TO ACT UPON IT.

If I were a woman I would claim John, chapter 15 in a personal way. Otherwise, only men can be saved.

When Jesus said in Acts 1:8, "Ye shall receive power, after that the Holy Ghost is come upon you," that promise was **for the women too,** as is proven by verse 14: "These all continued with one accord in prayer and supplication, WITH THE WOMEN" . . . "And they were ALL filled" Ac. 2:4. What for? To fulfill Acts 1:8 — "And ye shall be witnesses unto Me." That included both sexes.

Dr. Daisy Washburn Osborn

Anointed

Chosen of God

Commissioned

Preacher of the gospel

The T.L. and Daisy Osborn crusade attracts thousands of people from the nations surrounding Uganda, coming to witness what God is doing.

Dr. Daisy Washburn Osborn addresses over 200,000 women (besides men and children) on the historic Women's Miracle Day, in the Kampala Crusade.

JINJA ROAD, KAMPALA, UGANDA

Dr. T.L. Osborn and Dr. Daisy Osborn, "teaching and preaching the gospel of the kingdom" at the Lugogo Stadium in Kampala.

When we reflect upon the suppressed state of women under the Jewish system, and the fact that they were not even allowed near the worship area but restricted to the outer women's court, it is no accident that the Holy Spirit specifies "WITH THE WOMEN," and "they were ALL filled," so that they could ALL do the work of evangelism.

So, where do we propose to establish the limits for women?

Tradition says: "It is all right for a woman to teach a Sunday school class, or to even stand in the church and witness of what Christ has done for her, or to be a missionary, or to minister in a house, but she must not preach or teach."

But we must be careful lest we begin to split hairs inconsistently. For example: If a woman can go outside the church and witness, may she include Scriptures in her witness? If so, how many, before she would be considered to be preaching?

If she may witness, to what level may she raise her voice before her witness would be termed preaching?

If she may witness to one sinner, suppose a group gathers. May she witness to ten, or to a hundred, or to a thousand? At what point does her witness exceed the limits for a woman? How many may congregate before she must fall silent and call for a man to take over?

If she may witness to a sinner in a subway or in a private house, may she witness to one on the sidewalk, or in a park, or under a tent which she might decide to erect? At what point must her witness be forbidden?

If she may witness along a footpath, suppose a group gathers. May she step up on a boulder, so that others can hear? Suppose she witnesses on a sidewalk. May she mount some nearby steps and speak louder, so that others can hear? If so, may she mount a box or a chair or a platform? Precisely how loud may she speak or how high may she stand before she crosses the forbidden limits for a woman and intrudes the sacred domain of man?

If she may pray with one sinner, may she pray with two, or ten, or a hundred at a time? How many is too many for a woman?

If she may **witness**, may she **teach** or **preach**? What is the difference? Who is willing to split these hairs between **witnessing**, **preaching**, **teaching**, **evangelizing**, or **speaking**, so that the women can know whether they should obey Jesus Christ OUTSIDE THE SANCTUARY as much as they should obey Paul INSIDE the sanctuary.

Should today's army of cultured, educated, qualified, Christian women continue to remain silent in evangelism because of two statements made by Paul about a group of uncultured, uneducated women who were yelling to their husbands from the rear of the assembly about matters they were at that time unqualified and untrained to discuss? Must modern Christian women be restrained by that archaic custom?

To me, it seems medieval to handcuff an army of Christian women with an antiquated rule, restricting them from the worldwide ministry of evangelism, to muzzle their dynamic witness for Christ, when this

20th Century is decaying so fast and when thousands of strong Christian women would gladly go forth and do exploits for God if they were not held back by this formidable restraint. How can we, the Christian men, answer for the blood of millions of lost souls, who would be saved through the evangelizing ministries of gallant women of God, if they were encouraged to go forth.

I can't help but ask myself the question: How much of a sin would it be for Christian women to go outside the church building to evangelize and win souls — hundreds or even thousands of souls, even if Paul's orders to those uncultured, loud-mouthed women should be applied to modern educated women of this century?

I prefer to challenge the women to launch their outreaches for Christ in the same way that women organize and operate business affairs. And if it is a sin before God for them to win so many souls, then let their sin be laid to my charge. And I believe there are many other Christian leaders who feel the same.

Let us unite in prayer for an army of Spiritual Joans of Arc to sweep the world for Jesus.

One of the most significant Scriptures in the New Testament is in John 20:18. The "Living" translation says: **"Mary Magdalene found the disciples and told them, 'I have seen the Lord.' Then she gave them His message."**

I don't know why the men were not there the morning that our Lord had risen. They had heard His words. He had told them He would be raised. But they were too scared and too doubtful. But Mary Magdalene was there. She saw Him and He called her by

her name. She visited with the Risen Lord.

Jesus chose a woman to be the first person to proclaim the resurrection. Mary Magdalene preached the first sermon announcing that Christ was risen.

The Message of the resurrection is the heartbeat of Christianity. "If Christ be not raised, your faith is vain; ye are yet in your sins" I Co. 15:17. Ro. 10: 9-10 ties the salvation of every person to the belief "That God hath raised Jesus from the dead" and to the confession of that fact to the world.

The RESURRECTION is the greatest message of the church, and Jesus ordered a woman to be the first to carry that message. He said, "Go to my brothers and tell them that I ascend to My Father and your Father; and to My God and your God."

Just think: Jesus sent **a woman** to proclaim the greatest message of the church, TO THE APOSTLES THEMSELVES.

Can we forbid women to do what Jesus told a woman to do?

Shall we set limits on a woman's witness for Christ when Jesus chose a woman to bear the first message of the Church after His resurrection — the most vital and powerful message in Christianity — that "CHRIST IS RISEN"?

Dare we stifle Christian women or limit the number of people to whom they may witness, when Christ used a woman to proclaim the fundamental message of Christianity to the Apostles themselves — leaders of the Church? Mary Magdalene **"gave them Christ's Message."**

Can Christian women continue to be silent when so

many women in the Bible were messengers for God?

Do Christian women use Paul's words as an **excuse** for doing little or nothing in the ministry of Evangelism? Is it a **convenience** for their own lack of consecration and soulwinning courage?

Are Christian women willing to accept so many limits in God's ministry of Evangelism, when women of the world are asserting their influence and effectiveness in business, science, medicine, politics, and government?

If I were a woman today, I would not want to be regarded on the level of those naive, uncultured, loud-mouthed, untutored village women whose curiosity and ignorance caused them to blurt out questions or arguments to their men during serious public meetings.

If I were a woman, I would want to obey Jesus Christ **outside** the church at least as much as I would obey Paul "**inside** the church."

If I were a woman, I would want to be considered a Christian, a believer, a follower of Christ, a witness for Him, a messenger of the resurrection, a soul-winner.

If I were a woman, I would want to do the work of a Christian. I would want to realize that Christ lives in me; that He serves through me; that He speaks through my life; that He loves and ministers through me; that my body is His body; that He wills to continue His ministry THROUGH ME; that "As God sent Christ into the world, even so Christ sends me into the world" Jn. 17:18; 20:21 (Paraphrased).

If I were a woman, I would want to do the things Christ told believers to do, even if I had to suffer persecution for doing it. My Lord suffered for me. I would be willing to suffer for Him.

If I were a woman, I would want to be one of the wise persons who "heard the sayings of Christ and DID them" Mt. 7:24 (Litr), building my soulwinning ministry upon the rock of **faith and action**.

If I were a woman, filled with the Holy Ghost (Acts 1:8), I would want to be Christ's WITNESS "both in Jerusalem, and in all Judea, and in Samaria, and unto the uttermost part of the earth."

If I were a woman, I would rejoice because the prophet Joel said, "I will pour out My Spirit upon ALL flesh; and your sons AND YOUR DAUGHTERS shall prophecy" Joel 2:28, and because the Apostle Peter preached that "on my servants AND ON MY HANDMAIDENS will I pour out in those days of My Spirit; and THEY shall prophecy" Ac. 2:18; I would be so glad that the Hebrew word used by Joel means: Speak or sing by inspiration; to predict or to give a discourse; and that the Greek word used by Peter means: To speak under divine inspiration; to exercise a prophetic office; an inspired speaker.

If I were a woman, I would rejoice that Jesus never made a difference between the sexes. I would be impressed by the different women who were associated with His life and ministry. I would want to be like the lowliest one from Samaria who, as soon as she believed on Him, dropped her water pot and evangelized a whole city for Jesus. John 4: The people "went out of the city and came unto Him" . . . "and

many of the Samaritans of the city believed on Him" because of the testimony and evangelistic ministry of A WOMAN (vs. 30, 39).

Mrs. Osborn feels that women have a divinely privileged role in life. While they do not have to bear the full responsibility of the home, and are **always** to be subject to their husbands, in the Lord, they do however exercise an unequalled influence upon him and the entire home.

Someone has said, "The hand that rocks the cradle is the hand that rules the world."

My wife insists that motherhood is a privileged sanctity of life which exceeds the rewards and joy of anything a man may ever experience.

She sees the natural grace and influence of a woman as being excellent and rewarding beyond all virtues.

She says that women have an unlimited ministry, if they want to do what Jesus said to do: to witness, to win souls, to evangelize; their field is THE WORLD. She says: "Let no woman be preoccupied by restrictions imposed upon her ministry in the little corners of our world called the church buildings, when there are no limits imposed upon us OUTSIDE THE SANCTUARY."

The ministry which Jesus discharged to His followers when He went away, can **only** be exercised **outside** of the churches. Fortunately, for women, there are no traditions or Scriptures forbidding their ministry there.

So, the message of this book is addressed to women and men alike, to get **out where the sinners**

are; to get ON THE GO OUTSIDE THE SANC-TUARY, out on the busy boulevards and crossroads of society, out in public halls, cinemas, parks, in tents, in houses, in mobile homes, under trees, in theatres, and to tell the world, "I have seen the Lord" — then GIVE THEM HIS MESSAGE (Jn. 20:18 — Living Version).

HOW
TO
APPROACH
A
SINNER

J HAVE not written this book to teach soulwinning. That requires a complete study in itself. I have only tried to alert the church to the fact that tradition limits her ministry to **sinners who come to church**. Ninety percent of the unconverted can only be evangelized by taking the Gospel OUTSIDE THE SANCTUARY. Since we are commanded to reach "every creature" with the Gospel, we must take our message to the sinners, out where they are.

However, I do present this **one** chapter on **how to actually do the job**. It is only an **approach** to soulwinning — what a Christian can say to a sinner to draw him into an ideal conversation so that he may witness of Christ and salvation.

I present this in an attempt to show laymen how simple soulwinning is. Tradition complicates it.

Tradition holds that one must be a walking Bible if he expects to witness properly. Tradition obligates the laymen to be so competent in Bible knowledge

that he can rebuff any sinner, on any subject with "thus saith the Lord." Tradition imposes the image of a walking saint on anyone who attempts to be a soul-winner. Tradition complicates a very simple ministry. Tradition steals the richest blessing from laymen and reserves it as the exclusive privilege of the profession-als, who are usually very disqualified to do the job successfully.

The pastor of a large church told his congregation one Sunday morning: "You leave the witnessing to your pastor. Your place is to be faithful in the House of God." This is tradition!

Witnessing is a simple conversation between a Christian and a lost person about the plan of salva-tion. Any layman can do it. The big point is to get into the conversation without arousing opposition. If you can learn to do that, you can win sinners to Christ. That is why I have limited my counsel, in **this** book, to the technique of **getting into the subject**.

How many times have you wanted to witness to someone, but you just couldn't steer the conversation in the right direction. Rather than appear to be awk-ward, you let the opportunity pass.

I want to help you to wisely lead sinners into an ideal soulwinning discussion.

Here are a few very simple "approach sentences" which you can use in almost any circumstance to get the subject underway.

* * *

1st. "HAVE YOU EVER GIVEN MUCH THOUGHT TO SPIRITUAL MATTERS?"

Make the question natural, and thoughtful.

Its purpose is to center the thoughts of the lost person on spiritual values — without being too abrupt or direct.

You are striving for a natural, relaxed conversation. You may word the question where it will flow more smoothly for you. For example, after a few minutes of casual talk, you might say:

"We came to visit you because we'd like to get better acquainted. Mary and I have made a lot of wonderful friends this way. We've been Christians for several years and we've been so happy. I don't know what your attitude is about God, but we just never dreamed it could make such a difference in our lives. By the way, have you ever given much thought to spiritual things?"

Or you might be discussing your favorite hobbies and steer the conversation something like this:

"I'm glad to know about your interests. I guess that's the way we get acquainted better. Mary and I are Christians and we really have a happy life. Have you and your wife ever thought much about spiritual things?"

REPLY: "Oh, I guess we have. Not as much as we ought to, though." You can expect a rather general response. Some people may take ten minutes to answer; others, only a brief yes or no. Don't interrupt his reply. Let him talk. Listen. Size him up. Learn how he thinks. Your "approach" questions are only to get him to open up. Your time to talk is after the "approach" is made and the door is open. If you are a good listener to his

answers, you earn the right to be heard by him when you get to your real witness. IMPORTANT: Whatever his reply to your first "approach" question, long or short, **move to your next question!** You can only be sure of guiding the conversation if you stick to your "approach" questions.

* * *

2nd. "WHAT WOULD YOU SAY IS MAN'S GREATEST SPIRITUAL NEED?"

You are the interested inquirer, not the great teacher. Listen to his reply. He may tell you his own problem.

Stay relaxed. Keep it general. Your friend will begin to have confidence that he can discuss this subject without pressure from you. He may even bring up his own need of salvation himself. If he does, your "approach" has already opened the door.

You may reword this second "approach" question to fit the conversation more naturally, such as:

"You know, people are talking so much about our physical needs today, but our spiritual needs are important too. What would you say man's greatest spiritual need is?"

Or, "Most people don't stop to think that we have spiritual needs as well as physical needs. What would you say is man's greatest spiritual need?"

REPLY: "OH, I don't know; going to church and believing in God, I guess." You'll get all sorts of replies to that question. Don't interrupt them. Listen! It will give you a good idea of the person's attitude. No matter his an-

swer, **move to your next "approach" question.**

* * *

3rd. "YOU KNOW GOD TELLS US THAT MAN'S GREATEST SPIRITUAL NEED IS A REAL EXPERIENCE OF SALVATION. HAVE YOU EVER THOUGHT ABOUT YOUR OWN NEED OF SALVATION?"

You haven't assumed he is saved, and you haven't said he isn't. His answer should let you know. It will cause him to think about any time he ever had a religious experience, or was ever under conviction, or near death, etc. It will cue you in on his religious condition.

If he is saved, your question will still be taken well inasmuch as it opens the door for him to tell you about his own experience. But more than likely, his answer will be:

REPLY: "Oh, sure, just about everyone has." Almost always that third "approach" question will cause him to relate some incident. If he talks, LISTEN! Show interest! Then step right on to the fourth question regardless of his reply.

* * *

4th: "WHAT WOULD YOU SAY A PERSON NEEDS TO DO TO BE SAVED?"

Be genuine. This is the most vital question. His reply will tell just how much he understands the Gospel.

Amusingly enough, your subject will likely enjoy answering this question.

REPLY: Most unsaved folk will come up with one

of the "do-it-yourself" answers: "Always do your best, pay your bills, be kind to animals." Or "Go to church, be baptized and pray." They may even apply the matter personally and protest, "Oh, I never do anybody any harm. I'll be all right."

Notice, that with this fourth "approach" question, you are finding out if your subject is saved or not, without him knowing this. If you asked him directly, "Are you saved?" or "Are you a Christian?," he might say he is, then you could not question his experience without risking an argument.

Once a conflict of conversation develops, then you **might win the argument but lose the convert.** So avoid all dispute or conflict. Stay on ground where you can **appear** agreeable, but keep steering the conversation your way.

EXCEPTION: If your subject answers your fourth "approach" question with an honest confession of: "Well, I don't know" or "I couldn't say," then skip the fifth question and, instead, show him God's Word.

But usually your fourth question will draw him out, since most people have a definite opinion and will usually believe in doing good works of some kind. When he does give you his opinion, LISTEN to it! It's vital that you know what he thinks. Then go to your fifth "approach" question:

* * *

5th: **"YES, YOU'RE RIGHT. EVERYONE OUGHT TO DO THOSE THINGS. BUT WHAT**

I REALLY MEANT WAS: HOW DO YOU GO ABOUT RECEIVING SALVATION?"

    REPLY: Whatever your subject says, appear to agree with him that his idea is good (and it usually will have merit), but then go right to your sixth "approach" question.

* * *

6th: "YES, AND YOU KNOW, IT'S REALLY EVEN SIMPLER THAN THAT. COULD I SHOW YOU THREE OR FOUR VERSES HERE (CASUALLY PULL OUT YOUR NEW TESTAMENT) ABOUT WHAT THE BIBLE SAYS A PERSON MUST DO TO RECEIVE SALVATION?"

    REPLY: Your subject will usually say "Sure, go ahead," or "Of course, I don't mind." NOTE: Someone might say, "Oh I've read the Bible." Simply say, "Oh, I'm sure you have — and I'll bet you've found it interesting too. Notice here, these two verses." He'll look!

* * *

Now the door is open for your simple 5-point witness.

Don't preach.

Use no more than a few verses in one book of the Bible, as I've suggested below.

Make your points definite and aim for a decision.

I suggest these verses and this 5-point outline:

1. MAN'S NEED — Romans 3:23
2. SIN'S PENALTY — Romans 6:23a
3. CHRIST'S REMEDY — Romans 5:8

---

4. GOD'S GIFT TO MAN — Romans 6:23b

5. HOW TO RECEIVE — Romans 10:9,10,13.

(You can mark these verses in the margin of your Testament as a chain of references to follow in each conversation.)

In your "witness" period, **be brief and do not ask questions. State facts**!

Assume that your subject agrees.

Be positive and give the impression that you believe he is in full accord with everything you say and is glad about the facts of salvation.

Conclude promptly by suggesting: "John, these are wonderful truths. I know you appreciate how simple and easy God has made it for us to be saved. God says you must confess your sin and ask Christ to forgive you in order to be saved. When you do this, He comes into your heart and life. He really saves you!"

* * *

THEN SAY, QUIETLY:

"If you don't mind, I'd like to have a brief word of prayer with you."

Don't wait for his permission. Bow your head and close your eyes — and keep talking:

"While I pray, I'd like you to close your eyes and bow your head with me. Let's just imagine that the Lord is standing right here with us. He loves you and I know He wants to bless you and your home."

* * *

NOW PRAY:

"Lord Jesus, thank You for making it possible for us to be saved. Help John to see that he can be saved

right now. Help him to call upon the Name of the Lord Jesus. Save John right now, Lord. Let the real joy of forgiveness and peace come to him at this moment."

If your subject is a parent, pray for God to show him that his children need a Christian home. But be brief. Make it short and to the point.

* * *

IMPORTANT: Don't close your prayer. Don't say, "In Jesus' Name, Amen!" If you do, he will look up and your opportunity to get a decision may slip.

Don't close your prayer! Simply begin talking to your subject again, with your head bowed.

Say, "John, while your head is bowed and your eyes are closed, would you just ask the Lord Jesus to save you? You can do it right now. Just say:

'**Dear Lord, I confess that I'm a sinner.**'

Wait for him to repeat it. You've done all you can do. Christ is there. Your contact must now say "yes" or "no" — to Him. If he is being drawn by Christ's Spirit and if he has decided to follow Christ, he will begin to pray.

Sometimes, he may continue the prayer without further prompting. If so, join him in your heart. Or, he may repeat your first line, then wait. Be alert. Carry on.

"**I call upon Your Name.**"

"**Forgive all of my sins.**"

"**I believe You died in my place.**"

"**I accept You as my personal Saviour.**"

"**I believe You rose from the dead according to the Scriptures.**"

"I receive You into my life."
"I believe You do save me now."
"Thank you, Jesus, for my salvation. Amen!"

* * *

After your subject has accepted Christ, you can help him in many ways.

He will now have confidence in you and will feel that he can trust you. He knows that you CARE about him. He will likely be glad to attend your church now because he believes in what you have.

Arrange to take him to church, or be there at the door when he arrives. Introduce him to Christian friends and fellow church members. Take him to your pastor personally. Tell the pastor about his conversion.

Encourage him to **read the Bible daily**.

Share choice literature with him.

Visit him occasionally. Read the Bible with him. Welcome him into a Bible class. He is your brother in Christ. Before long, he will be going with you, visiting other sinners, learning how to witness, and soon you will have produced another soulwinner in your church.

* * *

Now for your convenience, here are the six "approach" questions to open a soulwinning conversation:

1. *Have you ever given much thought to spiritual matters?*
2. *What would you say is man's greatest spiritual need?*

3. *Have you ever thought about your own need of salvation?*
4. *What would you say a person needs to do to be saved?*
5. *How do you go about <u>receiving</u> salvation?*
6. *Could I show you three or four verses about what the Bible says a person must do to <u>receive</u> salvation?*

I suggest that these be **memorized**, along with the verses in Romans and the **5-point "witness" outline**. It's all any Christian needs to know, to go **outside the Sanctuary** and win souls for Christ.

"They that be wise shall shine as the brightness of the firmament; and they that turn many to righteousness as the stars for ever and ever" (Daniel 12:3).

Tools for evangelism provided for soulwinning missions around the world has, for decades, been one of the proven outreaches of the Osborn Ministries. (T.L. and Daisy, at center.)

19
OUTREACH – HOME FRONT

$\mathcal{I}$ DON'T BELIEVE IN fighting problems; I believe in getting on with solutions.

As we have ministered on mission fields around the world, the Lord has impressed me, from time to time, with **solutions** to some of the problems. One of those solutions has been the development and production of stockpiles of soulwinning 'tools'. These 'tools for evangelism,' as we call them, have now proved themselves in action for many years.

* * *

THE PRINTED PREACHER

Facing the need to communicate the Gospel in simple language, I wrote tracts in terms so basic that a child could grasp them — eighteen different salvation messages.

With the use of skilled translators, these have already been reproduced in over 130 different languages. Today, they pour from the presses at the rate of over a TON per day. They are so simple and biblical that missionaries of hundreds of Gospel or-

---

ganizations and missions use them and acclaim them as among the very best ever.

The Marxists have made their biggest advances in the world through the influence of the printed page.

The Bible itself is the Christian faith IN PRINT. We need no further argument for the value of the printed page.

I have come to consider the home front as another vast mission field, the pastors as missionaries, and the church members as national workers. This is why we make our soulwinning 'tools' available on the home fronts too.

These tracts, simple enough for a child, are equally effective for the most educated. The message needs no frills or intellectual jargon. No 'tool' has ever been invented which is handier or more direct in simple face-to-face confrontation in soulwinning than **the Gospel tract.**

A friendly smile, an offered tract and a word of testimony can open the door to a soulwinning encounter that can end on the knees in a sinner's prayer.

Equip yourself and your fellow-Christians with tracts, and you are on the first step to a soulwinning adventure.

THE MAGNETIC MESSAGE

One of the problems faced on the mission field is that the majority of national Christians find it difficult, at first, to tell the Gospel story accurately, largely because of lack of Bible knowledge.

I was challenged with the idea to help make it possible for national Christians anywhere in the world to do what I would do if I were in their place. So I decided to produce a 'tool' which would help them express themselves like an experienced preacher. With the help of magnetic tape, I could record the sermons which have proved most effective, and have them interpreted into any dialect by good interpreters.

By providing portable tape players (Lingua-Tape Units),we could make it possible for Christians to carry these messages to places never dreamed of.

Today that vision has been transformed into reality. Our tape ministry encircles the globe. More souls are won through our tapes than through our own personal ministry. And while souls get saved, the workers get an education. After they have listened to these messages several times, they begin to preach them too. Before long they can preach as effectively as I — and without an interpreter.

On the home front the same results can be achieved. Soulwinning becomes an exciting adventure when you arrive with your portable record player or tape player.

Think of Paul. He labored for days, dictating to a slow-writing scribe in order to produce a single epistle. He didn't even have carbon paper or a type-

writer. What would he have done with a good tape recorder? He would have done exactly what we are doing. He would have duplicated every message possible, sending it forth to the ends of the world to tell men of Christ.

Even Christian workers who are not preachers themselves, when equipped with sermon tapes or records, can witness to many souls and win them for Christ.

With our records and tapes, you can hold a two-week Gospel crusade in living rooms, family dens, parlors, jails, hospitals or even at the bedsides of invalids if you wish. (An earplug attachment eliminates noise disturbance in sickroom surroundings.) Amplification allows you to "preach" to whole groups — in homes for the aged, in the market place, or anywhere else there are people to listen.

And remember VACATION SOULWINNING! Many enjoy long periods of leisure, which they spend by the seaside, in the mountains, in the country, or even abroad. Among them, you will find thousands of souls who need the reality of Christ. These areas offer ideal opportunities to get out your tape player and your tracts, and show them the ONE WAY — Jesus.

Organize teams of personal evangelists among fellow-Christians, and inspire them to go out and conquer. With the help of these modern 'tools', any believer can amplify his ministry to win more souls.

A 73-year-old Ohio woman bought a portable tape player so that she and her 76-year-old sister could

visit the hospitals, the local jail, the county home and their shut-in friends with the Gospel. She wrote us, "I'm 73 years old on the outside, but I'm all new on the inside, testifying for the Lord. We old gray-heads can and **will** do something."

Every church ought to invest in a group of tape or record players for personal evangelism and lend them out to Christians with a zeal to work for Christ and a passion to win souls. How little the church has made use of modern technology! Yet it is here to be used.

In this arm of ministry we share our voice, our sermons, our soulwinning experience with the arms and legs and hearts of thousands of Christian laymen, winning lost souls and adding those souls to the Church.

* * *

20TH CENTURY FAITH LIBRARY

Books that bless and illuminate the mind are treasures beyond price. It has been my privilege to write and publish a treasury of inexpensive books on faith, salvation, healing and soulwinning.

This **20th Century Faith Library**, as the collection is called, is a faith-building 'tool chest' which enables the diligent soulwinner to prepare the hearts of his contacts, answer questions and clear up doubts, before or after their conversion.

They can be bought individually to be given or sold to interested persons (a liberal quantity discount is offered); the church, or any Christian can establish a lending library of faith publications, circulating the different volumes among converts and contacts.

If a book blesses us and we reckon it to be important, then we ought to share it with others. These books are available for just that purpose.

* * *

THE UNBEATABLE TOOL

No 'tool', ancient or modern, has surpassed the Miracle Film as a harvester of souls at home and abroad. We refer to Miracle Film evangelism as **the UNBEATABLE outreach**!

From countries around the world, reports are the same: Nothing draws the crowds like an OS/FO Miracle Film; nothing holds their attention like these dramatic **news** documentaries; nothing carries home the message with more force than these visual evidences of the power of God in action.

Filmed during actual mass Gospel meetings nothing like them ever appeared before, largely because no meetings, of such magnitude and miraculous content had been taking place in the age of cinematography. (I refer to the combined content of these miracle films: [1] travel interest, [2] mass evangelism, and [3] miracle evidence.) We pioneered these **all-fact, non-fiction documentaries** during the great Java Harvest crusade, and a new era of Gospel film journalism/evangelism dawned.

These films are not produced for the spiritual entertainment of church members, but to attract unsaved

and unchurched people to hear and to be convinced of Christ's power in this century.

Churches often rent a film for **one night**, as a convenient "fill-in" when the pastor may be tired or absent, or for other secondary purposes, but this is too limited.

The professional film industry always uses productions for a SERIES of repeat showings — **never for a one-night-stand**. Industry leadership is wise enough to know that **people tell people** what they see, and influence their friends to see too. Christian leaders must be, at least, as wise as the unconverted.

We emphasize that our DOCUMENTARY films are extraordinary in their impact on people's faith. Sinners — even atheists and cynics — find the evidence of God's power, shown on these films, very hard to sincerely question. We urge that they be re-shown at any given location, long enough for their influence to **penetrate the area for Christ.**

Remember, a DOCUMENTARY film has a totally different effect upon the public than a story-production with a plot or mystery which, when solved for the viewer, has no further attraction. **A documentary** will be watched more than once by the same people. These films are clear-cut CRUSADES FOR CHRIST IN ACTION. This is why they are ideal for Christians to utilize in attracting the unconverted.

These 'tools for evangelism' can equip you for many new outreaches. The documentary films can open the doors in scores of places where you might not other-

wise be welcome to minister.

During Summer vacations, at the beach, in the mountains, or on any campground, many will come and view the film — just to pass the time away. Once they witness Christ's power, they'll gladly stay and listen to your message to learn how they can know Christ in a personal way.

Our miracle films are also available, in most major languages, in ½ inch or ¾ inch VHS or BETA videos — in NTSC, PAL or SECAM.

* * *

OUTREACHES BEYOND THE SANCTUARY
Educational Institutions

In contemplating your field of evangelism, remember that these documentary films are extremely effective for ministry in schools, colleges, universities, summer camps, vacation centers, nurses training schools, orphanages, institutes of correction, boys' or girls' homes, etc.

The films will be admitted on an "educational" basis. You will usually be given liberty to speak before or after your film showing.

I cannot imagine a finer and more convincing tool for you to use in witnessing to the young generation.

Look at what the devil is doing with motion films! Think of the influence of evil being exercised today.

Let us influence our generation with Gospel films. We may be held responsible if we do not.

Public Institutions:

Hospitals, rest homes, old folks' homes, sanitariums and homes for the handicapped are wonderful fields for evangelism. Remember, even deaf people can **see** a film and the blind people can **hear** a Gospel tape or record. (One of our books is even available in Braille.)

There is a tremendous field of opportunity in the penal institutions — jails, penitentiaries, reformatories and labor farms.

And how about homes for unwed mothers, alcoholic and drug recovery institutes, government projects, military bases and special housing areas.

Have you thought about REFUGEE CAMPS?

Wherever there are groups of people of another nationality, you can find a mission field in your own home land. Our films, tapes, tracts and books are available in almost any major language you could need. (Spanish for the Spanish-speaking nations, islands and colonies; Urdu, Hindi, or Tamil for East Indians; Mandarin or Cantonese for the Chinese; Tagalog, Cebuano or Ilongo for the Filipinos; French for the French-speaking nations and islands of the world; Italian, German or almost any language you require.) You may have received a missionary call but never were able to go to the field. This is a way you can become a missionary on the home front and perhaps win more souls than if you had gone abroad.

And what about amusement areas, fairs and expositions? These offer remarkable opportunities. Lodges, factories, clubs, bars, houses of ill repute and taverns. Apartment buildings, street corners, parks, plazas, market places. On beaches, in mountain or ski resorts, at health spas, in organized vacation "villages" or camps. **Wherever there are people, souls can be won!**

These 'tools' can open the doors in wealthy residential homes as well as in the slums and ghettos of the poor. Rescue missions, Salvation Army hostels, flop houses and pool halls are more open doors.

You can show the films at missionary rallies, youth crusades, youth meetings and events; in halls or in other places where youth will congregate. As for young people on the move, youth hostels offer great possibilities.

With a Miracle Film festival as the center of your witness, your church can be mobilized to reach new districts for Christ, using OS/FO books, records, tapes, and tracts in house-to-house soulwinning. An invitation to a Miracle Film service in a neutral place will attract sinners who would never attend a church meeting.

Remember, active soulwinners are happy Christians. A pastor can inspire his people to go OUTSIDE THE SANCTUARY, to taste the joys of personal encounter and personal soulwinning.

I firmly believe that revival **inside** the church will result from a revival of personal soulwinning OUTSIDE THE SANCTUARY.

20
WHAT GREATER TOOL?

A FRENCH PHILOSOPHER said: "The public no longer looks to the Church for truth — they look to the cinema." He meant that the Church has become so much of a ritual that it no longer grips the attention of the new generation. Youth absorbs the philosophies of life through the medium of film. The result is a perverted, confused society in rebellion — not because the motion film in itself is bad, but because of what is shown on that film.

In 1947 the Lord Jesus appeared to me. I became convinced that the same miracles wrought in Bible days are for today; that only miracles confirming the Gospel would convince this generation that Christ is alive.

I then realized that in many lands, dead gods are worshipped because people do not know the Living God. So I set out to preach the Gospel to the unreached, overseas. I was persuaded that if the unchurched masses could witness the power of God to heal the sick, as in Bible days, they would accept Jesus Christ as Saviour and become devoted Christians.

We began going to country after country, to minister out in public places. We proclaim the Gospel, then we pray for the sick. Each miracle is proof that Christ is real and that His promises are true. Tens of thousands who were previously non-Christian are believing the Gospel and making public decisions for Christ. Multitudes are added to the churches wherever these crusades are conducted.

THE VISION OF OUR FILM MINISTRY was a vision to capture those great crusades IN ACTION, in sound, in color — to record those faith messages AS THEY ARE PREACHED and to film those miracles AS THEY TAKE PLACE, then to show those things around the world VIA FILM as a documentary witness that Jesus Christ is unchanged today!

Today hundreds of these documentary Gospel films are circulated in over 60 languages. Christian workers all over the world use them to attract crowds of thousands to hear the Gospel. They've proven to be among the finest 'tools for evangelism' yet produced for foreign missions and the home fronts alike.

These films are not religious fiction by actors, but AUTHENTIC DOCUMENTS OF THE POWER OF THE LIVING CHRIST IN ACTION. Evidence like these films is what our skeptical generation needs to cause them to believe on Christ.

The motion picture industry has warped and twisted the minds of millions of young people. Sex-

obsessed stars continue their influence on youth long after they are dead and gone, by means of film.

How much more should we expose the young generation to the influence of miracle evangelism — not with religious fiction by actors, but with documentary films which give proof of the Living Christ.

Modernism, atheism, skepticism pervade the atmosphere of most institutes of higher learning. Youth today who do not deny God outright, at least shrug off His existence with "What difference does it make?"

What greater 'tool' could be devised in this TV and film-minded age than the documentary newsreel of Christ's power IN ACTION, to reach out to the UNCHURCHED!

We have forged this modern medium of the motion picture into a major 'tool for evangelism'. Large secular companies are utilizing motion pictures to reach millions with their products overseas. The Marxists have proven the movie to be one of their most effective instruments. Hollywood has used it to saturate a generation with evil. Today the Gospel Film is one of the greatest 'tools for evangelism' ever devised — both at home and abroad.

The OSBORN FOUNDATION has provided these films to missionaries for years, in keeping with a policy of "Missions First." But the demand for them has increased so rapidly on the home front that they are becoming known as vital tools in the hands of pastors, evangelists, missionaries-on-furlough, Bible Schools or by qualified Christian laymen and laywomen, for greater soulwinning.

Mobile Units equipped with projectors, generators, miracle films, screens, gospel tapes, players and stockpiles of tracts are provided FREE to missions worldwide by the Osborn Ministries—for SOULWINNING.

21
TIME IS NOT IN OUR FAVOR

COMMON SENSE tells us that the Christian message is not being spread fast enough. For every soul won by the Church, 30 more souls are born into non-Christian homes.

The business world seizes every new method of promotion which is developed. Many "name" products are made available in the most remote areas — where the Gospel has not YET been preached a single time.

Many times we lament the spread of evil, yet there are fantastic possibilities for soulwinners if we simply apply ourselves to the opportunities. Many are so preoccupied with the closed doors that they become blind to the open ones.

Marxists have grasped modern media and developed colossal and effective techniques of propaganda, influencing entire nations. Films, records, tapes and the printed page have a much greater value to them than bombs, tanks, and guns. Their doctrine has al-

ready penetrated thousands of villages where the Gospel has never been preached. Why have the Marxists reached them so soon, when the Church has failed to reach them for so long?

The Church is not only faced with a growing challenge abroad. Bible faith on the home front is being honeycombed by atheism, and cynicism. From early school years right through higher education, the influence AGAINST faith in God is gradually increased until many young people from Christian homes return to their communities — atheistic at heart.

The astute Gospel minister reminds himself that the influence of this generation is relentless. TV and the cinema dump their poison into the bloodstream of youth every day. A clever 30-minute telecast produced by an atheist can destroy more faith in young hearts than the modern church can restore in a generation.

Time is not in our favor. Churches must be "on their toes" if we **care** about the unevangelized. These soulwinning 'tools' which the Osborn Foundation makes available, are TALENTS for Christian laymen, for evangelists, for pastors, for Bible Schools and for churches. Their availability means responsibility.

We had better not dream about opportunities for tomorrow. We had better act today and use what is available to increase our soulwinning outreach.

The man in Matt. 25:14-30, **delivered his goods** into the hands of fellow servants of God. I pray for every Christian layman, evangelist, pastor and preacher who is aware of these "talents" that he may

put them to work and "gain many more talents besides them," to whom His Lord shall surely say: "Well done, thou good and faithful servant."

"For unto every one that hath shall be given, and he shall have abundance."

May God grant that, whether you are a man, woman, boy or girl, you may discover fresh new soul-winning ministries; that you will JOIN THIS CHARIOT of Evangelism; that you will get on the go, outside the sanctuary, where the Holy Spirit will direct you to seeking souls who are eager for someone to guide them to the truth about Christ.

May your message proclaim Christ like Philip did (Ac. 8:32-33), until men will say to you, like the Ethiopian eunuch said: "I believe that Jesus Christ is the Son of God."

OSBORN CRUSADE—Calabar

22 THE REAL CHRISTIAN

Now I present this last chapter to you if you are not sure about your own salvation, or not certain that you have really been born again, or if you do not know if you are a real Christian, or if you have simply accepted a religion, joined a church and mentally assented to the Bible, without experiencing the new birth.

Most of all, I present this chapter to you who have never been saved or converted and know it.

The Bible says that we can *know that we have passed from death unto life* (1 John 3:14).

This chapter will help you to know, beyond a doubt, that you have experienced this inner miracle. It will take place in you while you read this with reverence and simple faith.

If you are already a Christian, committed to winning souls, this chapter can serve as a guide to help you show others how to experience the miracle of the new birth.

I want to tell you how you can be saved from hell, saved from your sins, saved from death, saved from disease, saved from evil.

You can be saved right now.

The Bible says, *This is a faithful saying, and worthy of all acceptation, that Christ Jesus came into the world to save sinners* (1 Tim. 1:15).

The Bible says, *God sent not His Son into the world to condemn the world; but that the world through Him might be saved* (John 3:17).

Peter said, *Whoever shall call on the name of the Lord shall be saved* (Acts 2:21).

You can be saved today. This is what you need: to be saved, to know Jesus Christ as your personal Savior.

But what does it mean to be **saved**?

First: To be **saved** means to be born again, to become a child of God.

Jesus said, *You must be born again* (John 3:7). This is a miracle. Christ actually enters your life, and you are made new because He begins to live in you. This is not accepting a religion. This is

accepting Christ. He is a person, not a philosophy. He is reality, not theory.

When I was married and accepted Daisy as my wife, I did not get the marriage religion. I received a person — Daisy, as my wife.

When I was saved by receiving Christ, I did not get the Christian religion. I received a Person, the Lord Jesus. My conversion was as definite an experience as was my marriage. On both occasions, I received another person into my life.

The Bible says, *As many as received Him, to them gave He power to become the children of God* (John 1:12).

What a marvel that one can receive a new birth and be born into God's royal family. You have been born once — born in sin, a child of sin, a servant of the devil. Now Christ says, *You must be born again* (John 3:7). You must be converted — be saved, changed, made new.

Second: To be **saved** means to have your sins forgiven.

The Bible says, *He forgives all your iniquities* (Ps. 103:3).

The angel said, *You shall call His name JESUS: for he shall save His people from their sins* (Matt. 1:21).

God says, *I am He that blots out your transgressions* (Is. 43:25). *And their sins and iniquities will I remember no more* (Heb. 10:17).

As far as the east is from the west, so far has He removed our transgressions from us (Ps. 103:12).

Third: To be **saved** means to receive a new spiritual life.

Paul says, *If any one be in Christ, that person is a new creature: old things are passed away; behold all things are become new* (2 Cor. 5:17).

That is exactly what happens when Christ saves you. A conversion takes place. Old desires, habits, and diseases pass away. All things become new. You receive a new life, a new nature, new health, new desires, new ambitions. You receive Christ's life.

He said, *I am come that they might have life, and that they might have it more abundantly* (John 10:10).

Fourth: To be **saved** means to receive

peace.

Jesus said, *Peace I leave with you. My peace I give unto you* (John 14:27). He said, *I have spoken unto you, that in me you might have peace* (John 16:33).

Real peace only comes with Christ's pardon and salvation. In sin you can never have peace in your soul. The Bible says, *There is no peace, says my God, to the wicked* (Is. 57:21). But *being justified by faith, we have peace with God through our Lord Jesus Christ* (Rom. 5:1).

Fifth: To be **saved** means to have fellowship with God.

You were created in God's likeness, so you could walk and talk with Him. But your sins separated you from God. Now, instead of fellowship with the Father, you fear God. The thought of facing Him frightens you. Your sin condemns you and creates in you a sense of guilt before God.

Only Christ can save you from your sins. He will blot out every stain and bring you back to God with a clean record — as if you had never sinned. Then you can say with the apostle John:

Truly our fellowship is with the Father, and with His Son Jesus Christ (1 John 1:3).

He will be *a friend that sticks closer than a brother or sister* (Prov. 18:24).

No person was made for a life of sin and disease. You were created to walk with God. But sin separated you from God.

Your iniquities have separated between you and your God, and your sins have hid His face from you, that He will not hear (Is. 59:2).

But, His blood was shed for many, *for the remission of sins* (Matt. 26:28).

If we confess our sin (to Him), *He is faithful and just to forgive us our sins, and to cleanse us from all unrighteousness* (1 John 1:9).

John said, *We know that we have passed from death unto life* (1 John 3:14). There are many things in this world which you may never know, but you can know you have Christ's life in you. You can know that you have been saved — that you are born again.

To say, "I don't know for sure if I'm

saved," is like a husband or a wife saying, "I don't know for sure if I'm married."

To say, "I think I'm saved. I try to be, but I'm not sure about it," is like saying, "I think I'm married. I try to be, but I'm not sure about it."

Jesus said, *One who believes* (the gospel) *and is baptized shall be saved* (Mark 16:16).

Paul said, *If you shall confess with your mouth the Lord Jesus, and shall believe in your heart that God has raised Him from the dead, you shall be saved* (Rom. 10:9).

These scriptures promise: *You shall be saved*.

Follow them, do what they say, and you can know that you have received Christ — that you have passed from death unto life, that you are saved! This is not accepting a religion. This is Christianity — the Christ life!

What is a **real** Christian?

According to the Bible, a real Christian is a person who:

1. Has come to God as a lost sinner;

2. Has accepted by faith the Lord Jesus Christ as personal Savior by surrendering to Him as Lord and Master;

3. Has confessed Christ as Lord before the world;

4. Is striving to please Him in everything, every day.

If you are not sure that you have personally accepted Jesus Christ into your heart as your Lord and Master, then follow these seven steps prayerfully:

First: Realize that you are a sinner.

All have sinned, and come short of the glory of God (Rom. 3:23).

If we say that we have no sin, we deceive ourselves (1 John 1:8).

Second: Truly be sorry for and repent of your sins.

And the publican, standing afar off, would not lift up so much as his eyes unto heaven, but smote upon his breast, saying, God be merciful to me a sinner (Luke 18:13).

For godly sorrow works repentance to salvation (2 Cor. 7:10).

Third: Confess your sins to God.

One who covers sin shall not prosper: but whoever confesses and forsakes them

shall have mercy (Prov. 28:13).

If we confess our sins (to Him), *He is faithful and just to forgive us our sins, and to cleanse us from all unrighteousness* (1 John 1:9).

Fourth: Forsake your sins, or put them away.

Let the wicked forsake their way, and the unrighteous their thoughts; and let them return unto the Lord, and He will have mercy upon them ... for He will abundantly pardon (Is. 55:7).

Whoever confesses and forsakes sin shall have mercy (Prov. 28:13).

Fifth: Ask forgiveness for your sins.

Who forgives all your iniquities (Ps. 103:3).

Come now, and let us reason together, says the Lord: though your sins be as scarlet, they shall be white as snow; though they be red like crimson, they shall be as wool (Is. 1:18).

Sixth: Consecrate your entire life to Christ.

Whoever shall confess me before others, I will confess also before my Father which is in heaven (Matt. 10:32).

But you are a chosen generation ...

that you should show forth the praises of Him who has called you out of darkness into His marvelous light (1 Pet. 2:9).

Seventh: Believe that God saves you by His grace.

For by grace are you saved through faith; and that not of yourselves; it is the gift of God: not of works, let any one should boast (Eph. 2:8,9).

Accept Christ Now

Now is the day of salvation, says 2 Corinthians 6:2. Not some other day — but now, this very day!

Behold, now is the accepted time (2 Cor. 6:2). Not some other time — but right now!

Seek the Lord while He may be found, call upon him while He is near: Let the wicked forsake their ways, and the unrighteous their thoughts: and let them return unto the Lord, and He will have mercy upon them ... for He will abundantly pardon (Is. 55:6,7).

The Lord is near you this very moment, so before you put down this book, if you have not yet accepted Jesus

Christ as your personal Savior, find a place alone with God where you will not be disturbed. Get on your knees and pray to the Lord this prayer right out loud:

—Dear Lord, I come before You to receive the gift of God which is eternal life. I acknowledge that I have sinned against You. I confess all of my sins to You, here and now.

I am sorry for my sins which have separated me from Your blessing, and I truly repent and ask Your forgiveness.

I believe on Your Son, Jesus Christ. I believe that, in Your great mercy and love, You sent Him to die for me, in my place. I believe He rose from the dead to live forever as my Savior.

I do, here and now, welcome Jesus Christ into my heart as my Savior from sin, from hell, and from all the power of the devil. I accept Christ as Lord of my life. Here and now, I devote my life to pleasing You.

Jesus Christ, You have said that, if I will come to You, You will in no wise cast me out. I have come to You with all my heart, seeking salvation and trusting only in Your blood. I am sure that You

do not reject me.

You have said, "If I will confess with my mouth the Lord Jesus, and shall believe in my heart that God has raised Him from the dead, I shall be saved" (Rom. 10:9).

I believe with all my heart that You are my Lord, risen from the dead. I do, here and now, confess You as my Master, my Savior, my Lord. I receive You now into my heart by faith.

Because You died for me, suffering the penalty which I ought to have suffered, I know my sins can never condemn me again. You paid the full price for my redemption.

Your Word says, "As many as received (Jesus Christ), to them gave He power to become the children of God" (John 1:12).

I believe that You do at this very moment give me power to become Your child. I believe that You forgive me now. Your precious blood washes all my sins away. You were wounded for my transgressions. You were bruised for my iniquities. The punishment I ought to have endured was laid upon You.

I know I am forgiven.

Thank You, Lord!

From this hour, I will read Your word and do my best to follow You and to please You in all that I think and do and say. I am now a real Christian, a representative of Jesus Christ on earth.

Now I know I am saved.

Amen!—

Daisy and I love you. God loves you and values you. Experience LIFE, HAPPINESS, HEALTH and DIGNITY as you GO WITH GOD and REALLY LIVE.

As an act of faith, register your decision by signing your name in the decision box that follows.

```
┌─────────────────────────────────┐
│          MY DECISION            │
│     Today I have read this chapter
│ on **The Real Christian**. I have
│ learned what it means to be saved.
│ I have sincerely taken the seven
│ steps outlined here and have rever-
│ ently prayed the prayer.
│     I believe I have received Jesus
│ Christ in my own life. I am now a
│ New Creature. I commit my life to
│ do my best to please God in all
│ that I think and say and do. With
│ His grace and help, I shall share
│ Jesus Christ with others.
│     Relying on Him to keep me by
│ His grace, I have made this deci-
│ sion today, in Jesus' name.
│
│ Signed _____
│ Date _____
└─────────────────────────────────┘
```

Seal your decision and confession by writing us a personal letter to tell us that you have accepted Jesus Christ and that

you have received the inner miracle of conversion.

We pray for every person who reads this book. Our greatest reward is to receive letters from those who have been saved as a result.

We will answer you personally, and we shall then become prayer partners in following and serving Jesus Christ.

Write us today, lest you forget. Tell us, in your own words, what took place.

We are praying for you.

— T. L. Osborn

THE JUDGMENT we deserved was assumed by our substitute, Jesus Christ, in our name and in our place, and that judgment can never be imposed on us again.

This is the crux of God's big love-plan in the Bible that we call salvation.

THE OSBORNS believe in PRAYER and MIRACLES! And God answers their prayers. Every day scores of letters are received from people, testifying to the fact that God performs MIRACLES — today — for those who have enough faith to ASK!

OSBORN CRUSADE—Embu

THE OSBORN
WORLD MINISTRY

The ministries of T.L. and Daisy Osborn have made an unprecedented impact on the world in our time. They are valued among the great soulwinners of this century.

Married at ages 17 and 18, the Osborns were missionaries in India at 20 and 21. In 1949 they instituted the Osborn Foundation — a world evangelism and missionary church organization.

Their **life commitment:** To express and to propagate the gospel of Jesus Christ to people throughout the world.

Their **guiding principle:** The top priority of the church is the evangelization of the world.

The Osborns have conducted mass crusades in over 70 nations, preaching to audiences ranging from 20,000 to 250,000 and more, nightly.

They have sponsored over 25,000 national preachers as full-time missionaries, reaching their own UNreached tribes and villages.

They have published gospel literature in 132 languages and dialects.

They have produced documentary films and crusade tapes for public evangelism in nearly 80 major languages.

They have provided airlifts and huge shipments of soulwinning tools for gospel missions and workers worldwide.

They have furnished vehicles with films, projectors, screens, generators, P.A. systems, audio cassettes and cassette players, and great quantities of literature for evangelism abroad.

They are energetic and prolific writers. T.L. Osborn's living classic, *Healing the Sick,* — now in its 29th edition — has been a faith-building best-seller since 1951.

Their big 512 page *Classic Documentary - The Gospel According to T.L. and Daisy,* is unmatched among Christian publications.

The Osborns have probably reached and led more unreached souls to Jesus Christ in non-Christian lands, and may have witnessed more great healing miracles among the masses overseas, than any other couple who has lived. Their team efforts in world evangelism are truly pace-setting as they proclaim the good news to the world: that *Jesus Christ is the same yesterday and today, and forever.* (He. 13:8)

OSBORN CRUSADE—Europe

THE OSBORNS, in national attire, arrive in Bendel State for another great crusade.

BOOKS
by Dr. T.L. and Dr. Daisy Osborn

BIG LOVE PLAN — 7/60 COLLECTION VOL. 2
FAITH SPEAKS
5 REVELATIONS FOR YOUR OWN MIRACLE
GO FOR IT — GET THE BEST OUT OF LIFE
GOOD LIFE
GOSPEL, ACCORDING TO T.L. AND DAISY
HEALING THE SICK — A LIVING CLASSIC
HOW TO BE BORN AGAIN
IF I WERE A WOMAN
IN HIS NAME
MIRACLES — PROOF OF GOD'S POWER
100 DIVINE HEALING FACTS
OPT FOR OPPORTUNITY
OUTSIDE THE SANCTUARY
POWER OF POSITIVE DESIRE — 7/60 COLLECTION VOL. 3
PRAYERS THAT BRING MIRACLES
PURPOSE OF PENTECOST
RECEIVE MIRACLE HEALING
RHAPSODY OF REALITIES
SEEDS TO SUCCEED
SOULWINNING — OUT WHERE THE PEOPLE ARE
THERE'S PLENTY FOR YOU
TWO-WAY TOUCH
WOMAN, BE FREE!
WOMEN ON BEAM — WINNING WITH ESTEEM
YOU ARE GOD'S BEST — 7/60 COLLECTION VOL. 1

For these and other titles, check with your
local bookstore or write to:

OSBORN MINISTRIES
Box 10, Tulsa, Ok 74102 USA

T. L. OSBORN

OUTSIDE THE SANCTUARY

CHRISTIANS ON THE GO . .
OUT WHERE THE PEOPLE ARE